Memorial Inscriptions
of
Dun Laoghaire-Rathdown
Co. Dublin, Ireland.
Volume 1

ISBN 1 8984

GH00372157

Published by
Genealogical Society of Ireland, Dun Laoghaire, Co. Dublin.
Price IR£5.00
(p+p Ireland & UK. IR£1.00 and others surface mail IR£2.00)

ACKNOWLEDGMENTS

We are very grateful to the following members who carried out this work on behalf of the Society.

Field Workers:- Barry O'Connor, Brian Smith and Sean Kane.
Typist :-   Barry O'Connor.
Layout :-   Liam MacAlasdair.

Our special thanks are due to the following :-

Rev. David G. Moyan.   Kilternan, Church of Ireland.
Mr. Ron Barrington.   Barrington's Burial Ground.
Mr. Tommy Rath.   St Brigid's, Stillorgan.
Sr. Francis Lally.   Dominican Convent, Dun Laoghaire.
Mr. Pat Kersey.   Dun Laoghaire College of Further
                        Education.(Ink Drawings)

CONTENTS

INTRODUCTION

The transcribing of memorial inscriptions is an integral part of the collection and preservation of records which are vital to the family and local historian. Over the years, the memorials of many graveyards have been recorded and published by interested Societies and Individuals providing a valuable source of information for the researcher.

The inscriptions in this book have been taken from the smaller graveyards located in the Dun Laoghaire Rathdown County area. While selected inscriptions have appeared in print form, this is the first publication to offer a complete record of all inscriptions found in these graveyards.

While words of piety and sentiment have been omitted, these inscriptions amount to a valuable collection of biographical details of those of the Protestant, Catholic and Quaker traditions interred in these graveyards.

A composite index, arranged alphabetically by surname followed by year(s) of death, name of graveyard and a reference number is provided at the back of the book.

"Inscriptions of Dun Laoghaire-Rathdown" contains the inscriptions from the following:-

BARRINGTONS :- A private burial ground situated off Brennanstown Road, Cabinteely. It has been in use by the Barrington family since 1824. There is a vault on the site which is surrounded by headstones.

BLACKROCK COLLEGE :- Founded in 1860, it stands in its own grounds on the southside of Williamstown, Co Dublin. A memorial to those who are buried in the College Chapel is fixed to the Chapel wall and includes the College founder Fr. Leman.

DOMINICAN CONVENT :- Located off Convent Road, Dun Laoghaire. This small cemetery was opened in 1849, two years after the main convent was established. Following the closure of the school and convent in 1993 and the building of the Bloomfields Shopping Centre, only the Sacred Heart Oratory, off Library Road, and the cemetery which is still in use, remain.

GLENCULLEN OLD .- Situated in Glencullen Village. It was in use from the 1820's until 1908. It is now closed except for those with burial rights. A plaque on the wall of the church ruin reads : St Patrick's Chapel, erected A.D. 1824.

KILTERNAN C.O.I.:- Located in Kilternan Village. The church, which has a very active community, was built circa 1816. It is surrounded by a well maintained graveyard which has been in use since 1841.

LOUGHLINSTOWN :- Situated in the grounds of Loughlinstown Hospital (St Colmcille's), Loughlinstown. A workhouse was opened on the site in 1841 at a cost of £7,600 to accommodate 600 persons. The burial ground was used mainly during the famine years. The graves are unmarked, and the inscriptions which were transcribed are from more recent times.

OLD CONNAUGHT :- Located on Old Connaught Avenue, Little Bray, was closed by Ministerial Order in 1948. It contains headstones dating from 1719 which surround the ruin of the old church.

RATHMICHAEL (OLD CHURCH) :- Located off the Ballycorus Road, Rathmichael. The ruin of this Medieval Church stands alongside the remnants of a Round Tower and is surrounded by headstones which date from 1724. The graveyard is still in use.

SAINT BRIGID'S C.O.I. :- Located on St Brigids Church Road, (Old Stillorgan Road) Stillorgan, which runs parallel to the Stillorgan dual carriageway. The small, well kept burial ground dates from early Christian times and surrounds the church which dates from 1706. The parish has a very active community.

TULLY :- Located at the end of Laughanstown, off Brennanstown Road, Cabinteely, There has been a church on this site since the 7th century. The church ruin is located in the centre of this small graveyard, which overlooks a nearby Megalithic Tomb.

Head stones which were impossible to read have been omitted. The numbers allocated to the plots and the index in this publication are reference numbers and should not be taken as plot numbers. The inscriptions marked with an asterisk in St Brigid's C.O.I., were impossible to read in full and the Society was able to complete these inscriptions with the aid of the unpublished work of the late Mr. Brian Cantwell.

Barry O'Connor.
Brian Smith.
May 2000

Barrington's Private Burial Ground

(Glendruid Cemetery)

Barrington's Private Burial Ground

(Glendruid Cemetery)

1 (Inside vault) This tomb contains the mortal remains of John Barrington, b 10/10/1764, d 2/4/1824 and those of Margaret his wife, b 25/12/1773 d 18/5/1869. A citizen of Dublin, he shewed his taste for the beauties of nature by planting and improving the surrounding Glen where she, during a long widowhood of 45yrs lived happily in the society of her children and friends.

2 (Inside vault) Erected by his loving children to the memory of Edward Barrington who died at his residence, Fassaroe, Bray on the 12/10/1877 age 81yrs. The inostentatious worth and dignity of his remarkable character gained him the affection of his children and the respect and esteem of all who knew him.

3 (Out side wall) Our mother, Huldah Barrington, 2nd wife of Edward Barrington of Fassaroe, Bray, Co Wicklow. She was the eldest daughter of Joshua and Anna Wakefield Strangman of Waterford and died at Fassaroe on 7/10/1895 age 75yrs and was buried in the John's Hill Cemetery, Waterford. This tablet is erected by her surviving children September 1905.

4 (Out side wall) Our mother Sarah Barrington, 1st wife of Edward Barrington of Fassaroe, Bray, Co Wicklow. Daughter of William and Mary Leadbeater of Ballitore, Co Kildare, died at Fassaroe, on 7/12/1843 age 45yrs. Interred in Friends Burial Ground, Cork St, Dublin. She left 7 sons and 4 daughters. This tablet is erected by her surviving children September 1905.

5 (Out side wall) Sir. John Barrington D.L.J.P., eldest son of Edward and Sarah Barrington who died at Killiney on 2/5/1887 age 63yrs. Elizabeth his wife, daughter of Jonathon and Eliza Pim who died at Killiney on 28/8/1900 age 81yrs. Both are interred in the Friends Burial Ground, Temple Hill, Co Dublin. This tablet is erected by their children.

6 Richard Grey Barrington, eldest son of Richard and Lena Barrington of Fassaroe, Co Wicklow, b 11/5/1900, d 24/9/1901.

7 Amy Barrington, daughter of Edward Barrington of Fassaroe, Bray, b 14/2/1857, d 6/1/1942.

8 Richard Manliffe Barrington of Fassaroe, Co Wicklow, son of Edward Barrington of Fassaroe and Huldah his wife and husband of Lena Barrington, b 22/5/1849, d 15/9/1915.

9 Anna Wakefield, eldest daughter of Edward and Huldah Barrington of Fassaroe died at Glendruid 14/6/1902 age 51yrs.

10 Alison Innes, wife of James F Byrne of Beechlands, Shankill, eldest daughter of Richard M Barrington, Fassaroe, Bray, d 24/10/1925 age 26yrs.

11 Marion Barrington, my sister who is buried here. She died on 26/6/1893 age 34yrs.

12 Lydia Sarah, d 29/1/1864 age 24yrs. Huldah Isabel, d 28/1/1870 age 18yrs, daughters of Edward Barrington, Fassaroe.

13 Richard Manliffe Barrington, 4th son of Edward and Sarah Barrington, b 29/3/1829, d 23/5/1847.

14 Selina Ffennell of St Margaret's, Foxrock, widow of Robert Ffennell of Banbridge, Co Down, and daughter of Edward Barrington, Fassaroe, Bray, d 18/6/1917 age 84yrs.

15 Charlie, son of Robert and Selina Ffennell, d 19/9/1882 age 18yrs.

16 Philip Sidney Barrington junior, d 29/11/1893 age 32yrs.

17 Selina Barrington, b 6/8/1805, d 17/9/1836. Emily Barrington, b 1/3/1809, d 2/4/1828, daughters of John and Margaret Barrington.

18 Erasmus Barrington of Maryville, Kilworth, 7th son of Edward Barrington, Fassaroe, Bray, d 9/3/1874 age 34yrs.

19 Elizabeth, wife of Philip S Barrington, d 16/11/1906 age 74yrs. Philip S Barrington, d 2/7/1913 age 83yrs.

20 Jane Kearns Deane, widow of Erasmus Barrington, d 9/4/1913 age 70yrs.

21 Margaret Lilian, 2nd daughter of P.S. Barrington of Ballyman, Bray, d 25/1/1915 age 47yrs.

22 William Bennett Barrington of Cork, son of Erasmus Barrington, b 6/7/1868, d 16/4/1928.

23 Eliza Bennett Manders, 2nd daughter of Erasmus Barrington, b 16/12/1870, d 2/11/1928.

24 Lucy, youngest daughter of Francis and Lucy Malone, died at Boherboy Cottage, Dunlavin, 23/9/1916 age 74yrs.

25 Richard Barrington, died at his residence Beech House, Red Hill, Surrey, 22/11/1890 age 93yrs. The last surviving son of John and Margaret Barrington of Dublin and Glendruid.

26 Bancroft Malone, youngest son of Francis and Lucy Malone, d 13/3/1907 age 62yrs.

27 J Reginald Malone, eldest son of Francis and Lucy Malone, d 2/4/1904 age 71.

28 Emily Malone, eldest daughter of Francis and Lucy Malone, d 7/2/1910 age 78yrs.

29 Francis Malone, d 16/1/1876 age 78yrs. Lucy his wife, daughter of John and Margaret Barrington, d 21/10/1871 age 69yrs.

30 My husband, Frank Malone, 2nd son of Francis and Lucy Malone, b 10/12/1838, *66 years*
d 2/4/1905. Owner of Glendruid for 24yrs having succeeded his uncle Arthur
Barrington January 13th 1881.

31 Marion Barrington O'Neill, wife of William O'Neill, Bonnington, Drumcree, Co
Westmeath. Daughter of Frank and Victoria Malone, b 12/3/1894, d 7/1/1974. *3~*

32 Victoria Barrington Malone, wife of Frank Malone, daughter of Edward and
Huldah Barrington, Fassaroe, b 16/5/1853, d 16/2/1947. Resided at Glendruid for
55yrs. *94 YEARS.*

33 Edward Charles Barrington, 2nd son of Erasmus Barrington, b 9/3/1872, *89 Y.*
X d 22/3/1961.

34 Annie Maud Barrington, wife of Edward Charles Barrington, b 9/2/1872, d 22/3/
1962.

35 Charles Eric Barrington, son of Edward Charles and Annie Maud Barrington,
b 4/12/1910, d 7/3 1994.

36 Hannah Ruth Barrington, d 23/8/1989 age 5mths.

37 Erected by his brother in memory of Arthur Barrington, b 19/11/1811,
d 13/1/1881, he secceeded his brother Manliffe as owner of Glendruid whom
however, he survived not quite one year.

38 James Henry M.D., born in Dublin 13/12/1798, died in Dalkey Lodge 14/7/1876,
his daughter Katharine Olivia Henry, born in Dublin 20/11/1830, died in Dalkey
Lodge 11/12/1872.

39 Eliza Henry, wife of Thomas Elder Henry of Dalkey Lodge and daughter of the
late John and Margaret Barrington, b 4/9/1793, d 1/9/1877. The above Thomas
Elder Henry, born in Dublin 14/7/1801, died in Dalkey Lodge 12/8/1883.

40 Erected by his brother Frederick in memory of Manliffe Barrington, b 6/5/1807,
d 28/1/1880. He devoted his life to his mother and during her long widowhood
was her constant companion. His chief amusement and occupation for more than a
half a century was the improvement of the lands of Glendruid.

41 John Strangman Barrington, younger son of Richard Manliffe and Lena
Barrington of Fassaroe, 16/8/1903 - 31/5/1971.

42 Martha Barrington, otherwise Gamble, relic of John Barrington, d 10/4/1876 age
67yrs.

43 John Barrington, son of John and Margaret Barrington otherwise Manliffe,
b 28/5/1800, d 18/12/1836.

Blackrock College

Blackrock College
Co. Dublin
(Holy Ghost Fathers)

A plaque on the external wall of the chapel reads as follows: The following members of the community are interred in the crypt of the college chapel.

1 Rev. Fr. Jules Leman C.S. Sp., College Founder 1860 - 1880, d 3/6/1880, age 50yrs.

2 Rev. Fr. William Ryan C.S. Sp., d 4/4/1874, age 30yrs.

3 Rev. Fr. John O'Keeffe C.S. Sp., d 9/5/1877, age 25yrs.

4 Rev. Fr. John Martin Ebenrecht C.S. Sp., Architect of the College and Bursar 1862 - 1896, d 20/8/1914 age 77yrs.

Dominican Convent
Dun Laoghaire

Dominican Convent

Dun Laoghaire

NB :- b = Baptized. e = Entered Religion. d = Died. *Italic* = Taken from Convent Records.

1 (Stone cross) Bernadette Morahan, Dominican Tertiary, Jan 1943 age 17yrs.

2 S.M. De Ricci Waters *(Kate, e 8/9/1859 age 16yrs, d 23/11/1900).* S.M. Imelda Connery *(Margaret, b 25/9/1898, e 8/9/1919, d 27/2/1985).* S.M. Kevin Cahill *(Mary, b 17/9/1848, e 4/8/1872, d 5/5/1932).* S.M. Pius Talbot *(Annie, b 4/9/1865, e 15/10/1897, d 5/12/1958).* S.M. Aloysius Burke *(Annie, e 4/6/1865, age 19yrs, d18/11/1917).*

3 S.M. Josephine O'Sullivan *(Lizzie, b 5/7/1858, e 8/9/1879, d 21/12/1940).* S.M. Martha Phelan *(Winifred, b Dec 1855, e 25/12/1877, d 8/1/1923).* S.M. Patrick Walsh *(Bride, b 15/2/1894, e 26/7/1919, d 30/7/1971).* S.M. Baptist Gowran *(Margaret, e 2/10/1853 age 21yrs, d 5/4/1899).*

4 S.M. Malachy McCormack, *(Bridget, e 31/10/1860 age 18yrs, d 12/5/1916).* S.M. Jane Martin *(Eliza, b 29/10/1854, e 8/9/1876, d 17/5/1946).* S.M. Pius Bourke *(Mary, b 2/6/1853, e 5/5/1874, d 29/3/1895).*

5 S.M. Stanislaus Forrester, *(Charlotte, e 8/9/1850 age 17yrs, d 20/5/1911).* S.M. Concepta Lynch *(Bridget, b 4/11/1874, e 5/7/1896, d 30/4/1939).* S.M. Cecilia Gallagher *(Mary, b 1/1/1890, e 19/3/1914, d 1/6/1969).* S.M. Dominic Benson *(Maria, e 26/11/1848 age 32yrs, d 16/6/1894).*

6 S.M. Osanna McCormack *(Anne, b 1/11/1856, e 25/12/1878, d 6/3/1888).* S.M. Brendan Healy *(Anne, b 1865, e 21/10/ 1892, d 25/2/1932).* S.M. Agnes Brennan *(Justina, b 14/1/1886, e 16/10/1904, d 14/3/1959).* S.M. Ann McCaffrey, *(Anne, e 3/10/1858 age 31yrs, d 26/8/1913).*

7 S.M. Antoninus Burke *(Alberta, b 14/12/1858, e 8/9/1876, d 28/3/1886).* S.M. Catherine Ryan *(Margaret, b 15/4/1855, e 15/8.1882, d 16/4/1941).* S.M. Baptista Hourigan, *(Mary, d 1995, no further details).* S.M. Vincent Dooley *(Mary, e 8/12/1850 age 23yrs, d 27/12/1910).*

8 S.M. Magdalen Bradley *(Rose, b 24/11/1846, e 19/3/1869, d 11/8/1883)* S.M. Gerald Holden, *(no further details).* S.M. Dympna Carty *(Margaret, b 1849, e 19/3/1875, d 18/2/1932).* S.M. Evangelist Ryan *(Alice, b 16/7/1872, e 2/2/ 1893, d 30/10/1949).*

9 S.M. Catherine Forrester *(Kate, e 2/7/1848 age 19yrs, d 19/3/1880).* S.M. Peter Bowden *(Elizabeth, b 13/7/1898, e 8/9/1919, d 11/7/1944).* S.M. Clare Francis Brennan, *(Clare, d 1996, no further details).* S.M. Columba Hammond *(Victoria, e 16/9/1855 age 18yrs, d 19/3/1910).*

10 S.M. Genevievre Phelan, *(Mary, b Dec 1856, e 4/8/1878, d 20/3/1929).* S.M.

Clare Dowley *(Ellen, e 28/5/1856 age 18yrs, d 2/2/1906).* S.M. Francis Horan *(Clare, b 23/8/1882, e 28/8/1902, d 14/1/1969).* S.M. Margaret Whelan *(Ellen, e 8/9/1857 age 19yrs, d 21/12/1877).*

11 S.M. Gertrude Doherty *(Jeannette, e 30/5/1852 age 27yrs, d 17/9/1906).* S.M. Martha Mackey, *(Anne, e 25/12/1860 age 21yrs, d 30/5/1876).* S.M. Maurus McHenry *(d 1969, no further details).* S.M. Reginald Power *(Margaret Mary, b 20/3/1865, e 8/9/1885, d 30/12/1938)*

12 S.M. Patrick Spolens, *(Mary, e 2/2/1851 age 30yrs, d 14/10/1904).* S.M. Rose Bligh, *(Eliza, e 19/3/1838 age 17yrs, d 14/5/1868).* S.M. Martin O'Brien, *(d 1990, no further details).* S.M. Teresa McKeown, *(d 1929, no further details).*

13 S.M. Augustine O'Donnell, *(Bridget, b Feb 1893, e 19/3/1914, d 8/1/1945).* S.M. Ann Gowran, *(Ellen, e 15/9/1844 age 22yrs, d 17/11/1857).* S.M. Gabriel Brannigan *(Kate, e 30/4/1866 age 19yrs, d 23/2/1908).*

14 S.M. Thomas Byrne, *(Joanna, e 7/3/1848 age 25yrs, d 15/4/1854).* S.M. Ibar O'Leary, *(Ellen, b 16/3/1888, e 2/2/1917, d 13/1/1926).* S.M. John Grimes, *(Margaret, d 1993, no further details).* S.M. Paul Martin, *(Ellen, e 25/1/1859 age 19yrs, d 11/2/1902).*

15 S.M. Thomas Murphy, *(Anne, b 12/3/1854, e 13/4/1873, d 25/9/1927).* S.M. Regis Kelly, *(Margaret, e 26/9/1845 age 23yrs, d 19/8/1856).* S.M. Agatha Cook, *(Anna, e 25/3/1851 age 25yrs, d 11/2/1901).* S.M. Baptist Knott, *(Brigid, b 30/9/1877, e 2/2/1905, d 26/2/1955).*

16 S.M. Alphonsus Murphy, *(Catherine, b 9/12/1849, e 2/2/1870, d 28/2/1925).* S.M. Agatha Moran, *(Teresa, e 4/8/1844 age 19yrs, d 6/10/1849).* S.M. Raphael Walsh, *(Catherine, b 8/9/1889, e 1/11/1909, d 1966).* S.M. Gonzales Kehoe, *(Mary Angela, b 2/10/1869, e 15/8/1889, d 10/12/1900).*

17 S.M. Veronica Kavanagh, *(Monica, e 1/10/1843 age 23yrs, d 3/9/1853).* S.M. Zavier Colgan, *(Letitia, b 10/7/1864, e 20/10/1885, d 14/4/1927).* S.M. Dominic Power, *(Louisa, 26/9/1876, e 5/5/1905, d 14/3/1953).* S.M. Dominic Purcell, *(Bridgid b 21/6/1874, e 15/8/1896, d 11/7/1901).*

18 S.M. Bridget O'Toole, *(Kate, b August 1846, e no date given, d 12/2/1933).* S.M. Ita Farrell, *(Kate, b 17/10/1869, e 21/10/1892, d 31/3/1903).* S.M. Paula Cronin, *(d 1987, on further details).* S.M. Bridget Foley, *(Anne, e 30/1/1849 age 22yrs, d 15/6/1854).*

19 S.M. De Chantel Segrave, *(Marianne, e 15/8/1850 age 28yrs, d 6/11/1858).* S.M. Ita Phelan, *(Brigid, b 20/5/1884, e 1/11/1907, d 26/8/1968).* S.M. Felim McPartland, *(d 1990, no further details).* S.M. Matthew Geoghan, *(no further details).*

20 Patricia Foley, St Mary's 1943, aged 15yrs. R.I.P.

21 S.M. De Sales O'Brien, *(Mgt , e 2/7/1851 age 23yrs, d 12/7/1885)*. S.M. Regis
Bardon, *(Teresa, b 18/7/1868, e 15/8/1889, d 24/7/1906)*. S.M. Albertus
McMahon, *(Catherine, b 9/11/1887, e 4/10/1908, d 21/2/1970)*. S.M. Laurence
Byrne, *(Margaret, 21/6/1873, e 2/2/1893, d 23/12/1934)*.

22 S.M. Gonzales Tighe, *(Ellen, b 15/4/1849, e 20/4/1870, d 19/12/1885)*. S.M.
Imelda Maher, *(Joanna, e 11/8/1851 age 18yrs, d 11/12/1908)*. S.M. Bernard
Whelan, *(Lizzie, b 26/11/1865, e 23/4/1893, d 13/3/1947)*.

23 S.M. Evangelist Collins, *(Mary, b 3/9/1865, e 8/9/1884, d 21/10/1887)*. S.M. Rose
Gilmartin, *(Mollie, b 10/12/1907, e 6/1/1927, d 30/11/1937)*. S.M. Vincent
Whelan, *(Lizzie, b 22/6/1893, e 5/4/1921, d 29/11/1979)*. S.M. Michael Burgess,
(Catherine, e 28/9/1856 age 24yrs, d 16/5/1910).

24 S.M. Benedict Brennan, *(Mary, b 5/11/1882, e 8/9/1906, d 17/1/1948)*. S.M.
Joseph Bourke, *(Anne, e 2/7/1849 age 22yrs, d 13/4/1911)*. S. Marie Archer, (sic),
(d 1991 no further details). S.M. Aloysius Peyton, *(Elizabeth, born 6/3/1865,
e 4/8/1885, d 13/3/1892)*.

25 S.M. Margaret Mary O'Keeffe, *(Teresa, b 6/1/1864, e 12/6/1884, d 19/6/1946)*.
S.M. Augustine O'Keeffe, *(Mary, b 5/10/1855, e 8/9/1874, d 18/5/1912)*. S.M.
Cataldus Laffan, *(Mary, d 1998, no further details)*. S.M. Alberta Hennessy,
(Anne, b 30/11/1864, e 8/9/1882, d 23/3/1895).

26 S.M. Magdalene Miley, *(Julia, e 15/11/1855 age 32yrs, d 28/4/1898)*. S.M. Angela
Cole, *(Mary Margaret, b 25/3/1860, e 20/9/1884, d 5/10/1938)*. S.M. Veronica
Flynn, *(Mary, b 25/3/1880, e 30/4/1902, d 30/8/1967)*. S.M. Rose Phelan, *(Julia,
b 26/12/1859, e 15/8/1881, d 1/3/1914)*.

27 S.M. Bertrand Butterly, *(Sarah, b 23/10/1855, e 20/4/1877, d 13/3/1922)*. S.M.
Agnes Petit, *(Mary, b 6/2/1849, e 13/9/1867, d 25/8/1898)*. S.M. Joseph Bourke,
(Anne, b 15/8/1891, e 1/11/1911, d 12/1/1946).

28 S.M. Francis O'Reilly, *(Elizabeth, e 12/4/1867 age 21yrs, d 12/4/1899)*. S.M.
Magdalen Moloney, *(Ellen, b 25/8/1875, e 22/7/1898, d 25/4/1965)*. S.M. De Ricci
Metcalfe, *(Margaret, b 30/9/1891, e 1/11/1910, d 30/4/1986)*. S.M. Hyacinth Daly,
(Ellen, b 23/8/1857, e 1/10/1882, d 11/9/1937).

29 Central Plot:- Mother Mary Aloysius Purcell. Professed in Dominican Convent
Cabra, 8/9/1831. Founded Dominican Convent Kingstown 10/7/1847. *(Mary,
e 24/7/1830 age 20yrs, d 18/4/1885)*.

A marble plaque lies near plot No 16 and reads as follows :

*I gcuimhne na ndaoine a fuair bas den ocras agus den anro a lean 1845
- 49, a mbas siud a chuig beatha duinn na deanaimis dearnad orthu.*

Written on the reverse side is the following : Sr. Agatha Moran was the last victim
of cholera in Dun Laoghaire. This cemetery was opened to receive her remains Rosary
Sunday 1849.

Glencullen Old

Glencullen Old

1. Erected by Laurence Rinkle ilm his father Mathew, d 2/5/1852, his mother Catherine, d 16/1/1878, sister Anne, d 30/11/1896. Grandparents Thomas and Catherine Dwyer and their sons Christopher, Anthony, James, Patrick and John. Their cousin Thomas Crosby.

2. Erected by John H O'Rorke Esq of Jamestown ilm of John and Mary his parents. Edmund and Bridget his brother and sister. John James Archbold, his only son d 16/2/1860 age 9yrs, his wife Cecilia Emily, d 20/2/1868.

3. Erected by John Flood ilm his daughter Sarah Flood, d 6/5/1898 age 19yrs. Elizabeth Flood, d 9/2/1904 age 11yrs. Mary Flood, his wife, d 15/7/1905 age 49yrs.

4. Hugh Roe, d 7/4/1865 age 84yrs. His son Cornelius, d 24/5/1867 age 34yrs, and two other sons who died young.

5. Erected by Hugh Roe ilm his father Thomas Roe, d 29/7/1890 age 81yrs, his sister Elizabeth Leary, d 26/4/1864 age 21yrs, his brother John Roe, d 28/5/1891 age 43yrs.

6. Erected by Bridget McManus, of Stepaside, ilm her father Christopher McManus, d 3/7/1863 age 75yrs, her mother Anne McManus, d 9/8/1856 age 69yrs. Her brother Christopher, d 28/4/1870 age 54yrs, her sister Mary McManus, d 1/9/1875 age 52yrs. John McManus, d 29/10/1918 age 63yrs.

7. Hugh Keeley, d 14/8/1906 age 69yrs, his wife Jane, died 1878, also their sons and daughters.

8. Christopher O'Connell - Fitzsimon, D.L.J.P. 1830 - 1884, his wife Agnes (nee Leyne). Their children Christopher 1867 - 1910, Richard 1868 - 1894, Daniel 1872 - 1948, Edward, died in South Africa 1873 - 1939, May 1871 - 1953.

9. Lieut. Col. Henry Fitzsimon, late 29th B.N.I., d 7/9/1865, his wife Marianne Fitzsimon, d 5/4/1899, their daughter Ellen Fitzsimon, d 7/2/1937.

10. Henry O'Connell Fitzsimon, b 13/4/1835, d 11/4/1902, Eliza his wife, b 18/9/1832, d 14/2/1901.

11. Erected by his sons ilm of Samuel Doyle of Stepaside, d 16/8/1869 age 60yrs, their sisters Sarah, d 20/6/1850 age 2yrs, Anne, d 26/3/1867 age 24yrs and their brothers Patrick, d 3/6/1883 age 28yrs and James, d 9/11/1883 age 44yrs.

12. Erected by Charles Doyle, ilm his son Samuel Doyle died July ??. John Doyle, d ??. Two brothers William and Matthew, d ??. John Doyle his son, d ??. The above Charles Doyle, d ??.

13. Erected by Patrick Daly of 56 Francis St, ilm his wife Mary Daly, d 20/8/1877 age 58yrs.

14 Francis Jackson, died for Ireland 29/6/1922. Ross Daly, d 6/5/1872. Cecila Daly, d 17/12/1892. Robert Jackson, d 22/8/1882.

15 Erected by Val'y Kelly, ilm his father Patrick Kelly, d 6/1/1827 age 73yrs, his mother Anne Kelly, d 11/4/1841 age 75yrs. His wife Cathrin (sic) Kelly, d 3/9/1849 age 49yrs, also his children. His daughter Mary Kelly, d 17/3/1850 age 26yrs. Bridget Kelly, 24/5/1929 age 58yrs, her husband Patrick Kelly, 12/7/1937 age 78yrs.

16 Erected by Michael Murphy ilm his parents Catherine Murphy, d 7/8/1827 age 36yrs and William Murphy, d 2/5/1852 age 67yrs. His brother John, d 7/8/1834 age 18yrs. A.D. 1856.

17 Erected by Mary Law ilm her husband James Law, d 20/11/1891 age 63yrs. The above Mary Law, d 13/12/1921.

18 Michael Cullen, d 16/9/1937.

19 Erected ilm our parents Thomas Kenny, d 12/5/1887 age 40yrs and Catherine Kenny, d 11/8/1927 age 85yrs. Our grandfather George Kennedy, died 1882 age 70yrs.

20 Mary Gaskin, d 26/6/1926 age 52yrs, her sister Katherine Maguire, d 22/12/1956 age 78yrs, their brothers John Maguire, d 20/3/1958 age 78yrs and Patrick Maguire, d 30/3/1965 age 81yrs.

21 Erected by Philip McGuire ilm his father Daniel McGuire, d 18/12/1839 age 70yrs, his sisters Bridget, d 18/4/1836 age 25yrs and Eliza, d 6/1/1837 age 30yrs.

22 Erected ilm of Francis McGuire, Glencullen, d 16/1/1892 age 52yrs, his father Philip McGuire, d 12/11/1896 age 86yrs. His brother John McGuire, d 23/5/1878 age 33yrs and three of his children who died young. Bridget McGuire, d 17/3/1921 age 72yrs.

23 Erected by Bernard Greaves of Carrickmines ilm his father Thomas Greaves, d 12/2/1840 age 86yrs. His mother Mrs Mary Greaves, d 17/4/1844 age 72yrs, his brother Patrick, d 12/11/1832 age 13yrs and two of his children Patrick and Margaret who died young.

24 Erected by Michael Gallagher ilm his wife Catherine Gallagher, d 19/11/1843. Their child Catherine Gallagher, died the 17th of the same month.

25 Erected by Henry Campbell of Ballybrack, ilm his wife Mary Campbell, d 28/4/1864 age 64yrs. His son Michael, d 12/4/1866 age 30yrs. His daughter in law Mary Campbell, d 26/12/1854 age 30yrs.

26 Erected ilm of our father Andrew Fitzachary, d March 1899 age 59yrs, his wife Mary, died March 1928 age 70yrs.

27 Erected by Mathias Fitzachary ilm his parents Andrew and Mary Fitzachary, Mary died 28/1/1828 age 50yrs and Andrew died 2/1/1838 age 69yrs. John C Fitzachary, d 19/5/1903. The above Mathias Fitzachary, d 18/5/1900.

18

28 Michael Cullen, d 14/10/1844 age 44yrs. Margaret Cullen. D 10/7/1866
    age 55yrs ?.

29 Erected by Denis O'Leary of Glencullen, Co Dublin ilm his mother Jane
    O'Leary, d 9/5/1838 age 30yrs.

30 Erected by Martin Hughes, Golden Ball, Co Dublin, ilm his wife Maria,
    d 22/6/1871 age 33yrs, his son James, d 1/8/1869 age 3yrs. His
    daughter Elizabeth, d 5/1/1879 age 17yrs. The above Martin Hughes, d
    26/5/1905 age 86yrs.

31 James Salley, Ballycorus, d 10/5/1923. Jacob Salley, d 23/1/1924, their
    mother Anne Salley, d 5/9/1930.

32 Mary Jane Carroll, d 8/3/1942. Joseph Carroll, d 12/3/1946. Bridget
    Carroll, d 25/3/1960. James Carroll, 19/1/1971. May Carroll,
    d 7/12/1979. (small plaque) our son Mark Riordan, d 3/11/1981 age
    12yrs.

33 Erected by John Roe, ilm his mother Bridget Roe, d 19/7/1849 age
    35yrs.

34 Erected by Mrs Anne McKeon of Kevin St, Dublin, ilm her husband John
    McKeon d 11/11/1876 age 42yrs.

35 Erected by Margaret Byrne, ilm her husband John Byrne, d 4/8/1904
    age 56yrs. My son John Byrne, d 8/5/1917 age 30yrs, also two children
    who died young. Margaret Byrne, d 26/7/1940 age 87yrs.

36 Erected by Mr Laurence Boylan of Classons Bridge, Co Dublin, ilm of his
    wife Mrs Mary Boylan, d 30/10/1861 age 39yrs. Bridget, daughter of
    above, d 8/10/1865 age 7yrs, his son Laurence, d 28/3/1877 ? age
    25yrs. The above Laurence Boylan, d 21/11/1879 age 70yrs.

37 Edward Campbell, died 23rd day of March age 48yrs. (no year of date).

38 Erected by Edward Farrell of Kilternan, ilm his daughter Anne,
    d 15/1/1855 age 25yrs.

39 Erected by Thomas Byrne, of Ticknock, ilm his father Laurence Byrne,
    d 9/12/1880 age 68yrs, his mother Elizabeth, d 6/12/1873 age 58yrs, his
    sister Catherine, d 25/3/1872 age 23yrs.

40 Erected by James Lenehan, ilm his father Patrick Lenehan, d 27/8/1870
    age 72yrs, his mother Margaret Lenehan, d 1/3/1862 age 54yrs. James
    Lenehan, Grange, Rathfarnham, (formerly of Ballybrack), d 30/4/1944
    age 77yrs, his daughter Mary, d 5/8/1919. John Lenehan, Woodside
    House, Sandyford, husband and father, d 14/3/1977 age 73yrs.

41 Erected by James Lenehan of Ballybrack, ilm his father James
    Lenehan, died Whit Monday 30/5/1898 age 68yrs. His mother Catherine
    Lenehan, d 18/5/1894 age 60yrs. Anne Lenehan, Grange, Rathfarnham,
    d 11/8/1944 age 76yrs. Bridie Lenehan, Sandyford, d 8/8/1994.

42 Erected by Philip Reilly, ilm his mother Anne Reilly, d 7/5/1854 age 78yrs, his father Bryan Reilly, d 25/5/1861 age 80yrs. Catherine his sister, d 20/7/1831 age 18yrs. Catherine (Mina) O'Reilly (nee McConville), Killincarrick, Greystones, Co Wicklow, d 27/2/1970 age 76yrs.

43 Erected by Luke Byrne, ilm his son Patrick Byrne, d 15/7/1832 age 18yrs.

44 Our mother Mary Carroll, d 19/12/1916 age 62yrs.

45 Erected by Charles Walsh, ilm his father Edward Walsh, d 4/3/1879 age 49yrs.

46 Erected by Rose Byrne, ilm her father Andrew Walsh, d 4/7/1875 age 88yrs, her mother Bridget Walsh, d 3/5/1900 age 85yrs. Her brother John Walsh, d 3/12/1866 age 14yrs, her sister Mary Conway, d 12/11/1876 age 28yrs, her sister Julia Fagan, d 17/9/1882 age 32yrs. The above Rose Byrne, d 2/9/1924 age 82yrs.

47 Erected by Mr Laurence McEneny, ilm his wife Anne, d 18/2/1859 age 33yrs, his mother Julia McEneny, d 26/1/1855 age 65yrs, his father John McEneny, d 6/1/1839 age 60yrs, his brother Patrick McEneny died December 1838 age 26yrs.

48 Erected by Mary Doyle, ilm her father William McAnany, d 15/1/1876 age 74yrs, her brother Patrick, d 20/11/1878 age 38yrs, her mother Margaret, d 24/2/1881 age 74yrs.

49 Erected by Michael Kenny, ilm his mother Rebecca Kenny, d 3/12/1889 age 39yrs, his father, Robert Kenny, d 7/3/1905 age 61yrs.

50 Erected by Thomas Kenney, ilm his wife Anne, d 14/6/1892 age 40yrs, his daughter Catherine, d 16/8/1895 age 12yrs, his mother Catherine, died September 1855 age 38yrs, his brother John, d 20/8/1875 age 30yrs.

51 Laurence Caulin, d 17/6/1878 age 83yrs ?.

52 Erected by Peter Byrne, ilm his mother Mary Byrne, d 7/2/1870 age 63yrs, his father John Byrne, 1/9/1873 age 67yrs, his brother John, d 26/10/1853 age 14yrs, his brother James, d 19/12/1877 age 43yrs.

53 Erected by William Licken, ilm his father, mother and relatives. His wife Mary Licken, d 3/4/1917. The above William Licken, d 31/1/1938.

54 Owen Licken, d 30/10/1938. Christina Licken, d 16/9/1961. Owen Licken, d 19/4/1953. Thomas Licken, d 5/10/1988.

55 Bridget Byrne, d 23/10/1915 ? age 30yrs ?. Her husband Philip Byrne, d 21/4/1938 ? age 47yrs.

56 Our father John Merrigan, d 14/7/1915 age 57yrs, our mother Ellen Merrigan, d 2/12/1931 age 76yrs.

57 Erected by Peter and Mary Flanagan, ilm their children, John, d 30/5/1915 age 21yrs. Rosie, d 31/5/1915 age 17yrs, Peter, d 6/6/1915 age 19yrs. Peter Flanagan, d 25/8/1930 age 68yrs.

58 Erected by Mary Mulligan, ilm her husband Hugh Mulligan, d 16/5/1915 age 60yrs. Christopher Mulligan, d 31/8/1933 age 30yrs. Kathleen Mulligan, Killegar, Enniskerry, d 22/5/1965.

59 Margaret Mulligan of Carrickmines, d 30/4/1895, her husband Patrick Mulligan, d 20/7/1895, her daughter Esther Hackett of Carrickmines, d 16/5/1942. Baby Hackett, d 27/3/1963.

60 Erected by James Clarke of Carrickmines ilm his father James Clarke, d 17/2/1864 age 65yrs, his mother Elizabeth, d 26/9/1858 age 63yrs and three of their children.

61 John Farrell, Glencullen Rd, d 20/9/1933.

62 Laurence Roe, Jamestown House, Kilternan, d 8/10/1947 age 63yrs, his wife Agnes, d 4/6/1977 age 94yrs.

63 Our mother Margaret Donnelly, 4 Charlemont Row, Dublin, d 27/10/1918 age 69yrs. Our father, Michael Donnelly, d 19/11/1892 age 45yrs, our brother Peter who died young. Their son Patrick J Donnolly, d 19/2/1927 age 54yrs.

64 Catherine Kinsella, Ballyogan Rd, Carrickmines, d 27/7/1952 age 80yrs, our father Thomas Kinsella, d 30/3/1958.

65 Thomas Kenny, d 17/10/1927 age 79yrs, his wife Bridget Kenny, d 20/2/1916 age 65yrs.

66 Honor Pierce, d 4/6/1916.

67 Edward and Bridget Byrne. (no dates).

68 Catherine Roe, d 19/4/1940 age 53yrs, her husband James, 18/12/1982 age 95yrs, their sons Pat and Jim.

69 Michael Roe of Woodside, d 9/2/1918 age 55yrs. Elizabeth Roe, d 9/8/1916 age 16yrs. His wife Margaret, d 25/2/1953, their daughter Margaret, d 27/12/1975.

70 Peter Travers formerly of Harolds Grange, Rathfarnham, d 10/12/1897 age 63yrs. Jane Travers, d 2/3/1919 age 89yrs. Thomas Travers, d 2/11/1914 age 23yrs. Peter Travers, d 22/11/1923 age 38yrs. Elizabeth, d 11/1/1929 age 20yrs. Their mother Margaret Travers, d 5/4/1931 age 70yrs. Margaret Travers, d 15/9/1931 age 69yrs. Peter Travers, 30/4/1942 age 78yrs. Mary Jane Travers, d 8/6/1951 age 84yrs. Patrick Travers, d 8/7/1945 age 64yrs.

71 James Kinsella, d 17/5/1944 age 67yrs, his wife Mary, d 5/4/1966 age 94yrs. Ellen Kinsella who died young.

72 Denis Gallagher, 4 Elm Pk Terrace, Terenure, Co Dublin, d 13/6/1923 age 68yrs, his wife Catherine Gallagher, d 4/2/1939. Their son William, d 20/8/1976.

73 Margaret Walsh, d 14/12/1917 age 65yrs.

74 My mother Juila Hocarty, d 21/2/1900, my father Patrick Hocarty, d 27/3/1927.

75 James Salley, d 19/1/1917 ?, his son John Salley, d 18/4/1919, his daughter Mrs Ellen O'Neill, d 25/2/1922.

76 Erected by wife and family of Peter Walsh, d 14/11/1933 age 66yrs ?, his wife Bridget Walsh, d 23/1/1951 age 78yrs.

77 Edward Kerr, d 14/5/1928 ?, his mother Kate, d 23/1/1931 ?.

78 Michael Cullen, d 22/3/1920. John Leo, d 31/5/1946. Alice, d 10/11/1973.

79 Patrick Ellis, d 17/1/1946.

80 Andrew Ward, d 17/1/1917. Mary Ward, d 12/8/1921.

81 Our parents, Edward Thomas, d 14/8/1922. Annie Thomas, d 1/3/1959.

82 Patrick McCann, d 23/11/1921 age 40yrs.

83 Our father John Kenny, d 23/4/1928 age 74yrs, his sons John, d 7/6/1940, Laurence, d 16/3/1946.

84 Elizabeth O'Neill, d 2/6/1925. Patrick O'Neill, d 13/8/1944 ?.

85 John O'Neill, d 9/8/1920 age 71yrs.

86 Our father William Carroll, d 20/11/1924 age 71yrs. Grandson Patrick, d 2/3/1929 age 5 ½ yrs. His son William Carroll, d 16/2/1951 age 71yrs.

87 Pat Hayden late of the Scalp, d 17/5/1966, his wife Eleanor Hayden, d 9/11/1991.

88 Erected by Bridget Stokes ilm her husband Henry Stokes of Stepaside, d 4/6/1876 age ?.

89 Peter Dolan, d 17/8/1920.

90 James Doyle, d 1/4/1926 age 52yrs, his wife Anne Doyle, d 7/10/1938 ? age 60yrs.

91 Betty Mulvey, d 18/6/1945 age 21yrs.

92 Peter Boylan, d 8/4/1953 age 90yrs, his wife Margaret Boylan, d 25/1/1956 age 81yrs. Peter, youngest son of above, d 1/4/1925.

93 Robert Daly, 3 Kellystown, Ticknock, d 28/6/1984 age 68yrs, his parents Jane Daly died May 1923, Robert Daly, died December 1946.

94 John Moore, d 3/5/1924 age 25yrs, his mother Catherine Moore, d 20/6/1952 age 75yrs, his father John Moore, d 31/1/1954 age 78yrs.

95 Our mother Mary Byrne, d 9/4/1879, our father Richard, d 14/1/1890, brothers Sylvester, d 20/3/1946, Richard, d 14/9/1903 and James, d 13/3/1920.

96 Rev Patrick Smyth, PP of Sandyford and Glencullen, ordained 1815, to this parish 1828 died 28/5/1860.

97 Our children, Patrick, d 7/1/1938 age 21yrs. Kathleen, d 25/6/1929 age 2yrs. Maureen, d 6/10/1938 age 1yr. Erected by their parents Patrick and Annie Carroll.

98 Erected by James Toole ilm his father James, d 15/5/1857 age 74yrs.

99 My parents Mary Anne Murphy, d 20/8/1920 age 54yrs, Patrick Murphy, d 15/3/1922 age 58yrs, brother William, d 28/1/1906 age 15yrs.

100 Alexander McCann, d 7/7/1900 age 69yrs, wife Annie McCann, d 23/3/1919 age 75yrs. John Byrne, son in law, d 12/7/1926 age 62yrs. Catherine wife of the above, d 1/11/1941.

101 Erected by Julia Glynn, Goldenball, ilm her husband Thomas Glynn, d 5/3/1894. Her sister Jane Flood, d 4/6/1898.

102 Erected by Charles O'Neill ilm his mother Eliza O'Neill, d 20/3/1876, also ???. (stone embedded).

103 Father, Peter O'Neill, d 11/4/1852 age 52yrs, mother Rose O'Neill, died 1842 age 56yrs. (no month given), son John O'Neill, d 17/2/1902 age 73yrs, his wife Julia O'Neill, d 26/5/1920 age 85yrs, his daughter Margaret O'Neill, d 19/2/1887 age 10yrs.

104 Mother Mary Doyle, a 76yrs ?, d 22/5/1902. Son Joseph, d 22/9/1906 ? a 7yrs. Daughter Isabella, d 22/91907 age 3yrs ? also Katie, d 10/4/1917 age ?.

105 Parents John Nolan, Ticknock, d 27/9/1908 age 64yrs, wife Catherine, d 16/5/1905 age 56yrs, sister Mary Ellen, d 19/11/1896 age 17yrs. Uncle Peter Nolan, d 26/3/1910 age 73yrs. John Nolan, d 15/2/1930, his wife Bridget, d 18/7/1973, late of Jamestown House.

106 Our parents, Patrick O'Brien, d 31/10/1911 age 73yrs and Jane O'Brien, d 8/5/1912 age 65yrs, sister Jane Davitt, d 13/5/1902 age 22yrs.

107 William Byrne, Murphystown, husband of Ellen Byrne, d 12/3/1903, son Joseph Byrne, d 8/6/1909. Ellen wife of William, d 16/3/1919. Julia Byrne, d 21/6/1949. Rosanna Byrne, d 23/3/1954. Elizabeth Byrne, d 18/7/1963.

108 My wife Jane McCluskey, d 28/9/1915 age 43yrs, daughter Kathleen, d 20/5/1922 age 12yrs. The above John McCluskey, d 18/6/1940 age 68yrs.

109 Margaret McDonagh, d 11/6/1914.

110 Patrick Maher, d 16/8/1897 age 68yrs, son Patrick, d 28/6/1875 age 11yrs, wife Anne, d 10/6/1911 age 72yrs.

111 Mary Martin, d 1/4/1899 age 71yrs, husband Edward Martin, d 11/9/1906 age 79yrs.

112 Catherine Nolan, d 27/7/1902.

113 Our parents Jane O'Neill, d 14/3/1847 age 67yrs, father John O'Neill, d 23/1/1864 age 83yrs. Four children who died young Jane, John, Patrick and Patrick. (two of the same name). Maria O'Neill, d 23/10/1877 age 20yrs. Anne O'Neill, d 5/5/1880 age 57yrs.

114 My husband Patrick Mulligan, d 1/8/1946 age 82yrs, son Edward, d 30/1/1915. The above Mary Mulligan, 24/2/1958 age 87yrs. Cecilia, daughter of Patrick and Mary Mulligan, d 19/8/1975.

115 Peter McCabe, 9/6/1904 age 70yrs, his wife Elizabeth, d 17/11/1904 age 68yrs. Annie McCabe, d 16/5/1912 age 1yr 9mths. Bridget McCabe, d 29/1/1938.

116 Erected by James Butler ilm his wife and family, Andrew, died March 1895. John died August 1901. James died December 1902. Bridget died August 1909. Andrew died September 1916. Maryann died January 1917.

117 Laurence and Annie Walsh. (no dates).

118 Mother- Mary McCabe died aged 62yrs. Sister - Ellen died aged 17yrs. Brother - James. Erected by John McCabe.

119 My wife Mary, d 15/6/1928 age 44yrs, my father Michael, d 25/9/1900 age 70yrs, mother Mary, d 12/5/1895 age 58yrs. Erected by Terence Maguire.

120 John McGinn, died July 1936.

121 Erected by James Doyle ilm his wife Anne, d 1/9/1868 age 46yrs.

122 Parents - John Walsh, 5/12/1950 his wife Catherine, d 8/8/1939. Children Patrick and Rose who died young. Son Michael (Mick), d 20/4/1995 age 82yrs.

123 Michael and Matthew Power. Erected by Adam Power.

124 Erected by John Connor ilm his sons, Philip, d 19/4/1920 age 3mths and Thomas, died October 1920 age 8yrs.

125 Erected by Bridget Kelly ilm her father Michael Kelly, d 5/12/1899 age 62yrs, mother Bridget Kelly, d 7/4/1950 age 83yrs also her brother Martin.(no date).

126 William Latten, b 4/5/1881, d 4/3/1910.

127 Erected by Margaret Byrne of Clanbrassil St, Dublin ilm her mother Margaret Byrne, d 18/9/1909 age 74yrs, father John Byrne, d 10/2/1910 age 79yrs.

128 My wife Margaret (Peggy) Savage, d 22/11/1951, her father Richard Ryan, d 3/11/1926, her sister Molly Ryan, d 6/6/1932, her mother Mary Ryan, d 14/2/1956. George Savage, husband of Peggy, d 31/1/1988.

129 Valentine Byrne, 4/3/1953 ?. Kathleen Byrne, d 22/11/1953, son John, d 7/7/1910.

130 Fox - daughter Mary Polly, d 17/5/1907 age 16yrs. John Fox, d 20/10/1911 age 53yrs. Son - James, d 11/8/1926 age 25yrs. William, d 8/6/1930 age 38yrs. Their mother Bridget, d 11/3/1939 age 78yrs.

131 Erected by her nieces ilm of Mary McManus late Frankfort, Rathgar, d 18/11/1921 ?, husband James died January 1903 ?.

132 Charles McManus, d 23/6/1921 age 66yrs. Erected by his wife.

133 Erected by William Field of Killgobin, Co Dublin ilm his daughter Mary Field, d 19/7/1830 age 17yrs.

134 Erected by John Dunne ilm his wife Mary, died January 1881 age 66yrs. Alexander Fleming, d 19/10/1898.

135 Wife - Mary, d 2/3/1919 age 67yrs. Husband - Hugh, d 26/8/1926 age 85yrs, son Thomas, 19/11/1939 age 64yrs. Catherine Roe, d 27/7/1951 ?. Margaret Roe, d ?/10/1958. Bridget Doyle, d 25/2/1958.

136 Erected by Walter Kelly of Ballyedmonduff ilm his sister Anne Kelly, d 23/4/1835 age 21yrs, his wife Anne, d 27/6/1847 age 32yrs, his mother Jane, d 27/2/1848 age 86yrs.

137 Erected by 2nd eldest daughter Jane ilm her parents William Kelly of Ballyedmonduff, Dublin, d 27/7/1847 age 49yrs and Mary Kelly, d 9/9/1871 age 70yrs. Their children Ann, Felise, Walter and Felix who died young. William, died 1879 age 27yrs. Ellen, d 28/10/1889 age 68yrs.

138 Parents - Peter Walsh, 12/7/1940 and Esther Walsh, d 24/10/1947. Their relatives who are interred in this grave.

139 Erected by his fellow members of Glencullen Band ilm of John Bradshaw, d 17/5/1910 age 58yrs.

Kilternan

Kilternan

1   Erected by Elizabeth Harding ilm her parents John Harding, d 10/9/1919 age 71yrs, Anne Harding, d 23/4/1916 age 82yrs.

2   Warren Storey MIEE. MICE. (I), d 16/2/1952. Esther Storey, d 20/2/1961.

3   Sidney Howard Guilford, d 28/4/1953, his wife Caroline Edith, d 4/3/1966.

4   Martha Power, d 18/4/1970.

5   Benjamin B Russell, killed in Manx Grand Prix at Lezayre, 9/9/1947. May Elizabeth Russell, d 29/3/1955. George Alexander Russell, d 27/12/1956.

6   James East, formerly of Fort Louis, Sligo, d 23/2/1950. His wife Eleanor, d 22/1/1951, his son J Sidney East of Clonskeagh, Dublin 1911-1991.

7   Arthur Cowan Digby French, Priest 1876-1950. Synolda Georgina, his wife, 1881-1971. Robert Butler Digby French, 1904-1981. Eleanor (Nell) Digby French, 1906-1992.

8   Arthur Joseph Thompson, d 27/11/1951 age 49yrs. His son Alan David, died September 1963 age 17yrs. Frances E Thompson, (nee Mercier), wife of Arthur, d 10/4/1990.

9   Isobel H M Downs, d 19/5/1975. Robert W Downs, d 29/9/1978.

10 Gladys Ross, d 14/9/1990.

11 Agnes Grace (Queenie) Stewart, daughter of Captain and Mrs Hugh Stewart, Hatlex, Foxrock, Co Dublin, died September 1950. Harriet Amy (Harrie), d 4/6/1965. Mary (May) Stewart RRC. OAIMNS., d 30/12/1969 age 94yrs.

12 Frances Jane Hilton (nee Richardson), d 6/1/1952 age 75yrs wife and mother. John Hilton, d 22/3/1956 age 83yrs husband and father.

13 Victoria A E Wilson, wife of J Hugh Wilson, Carrickmines House, Carrickmines, d 6/1/1928 ?. Gwendoline A S Wilson (Birdie) wife of J Hugh Wilson, late of Carrickmines, d 25/7/1955 ?. J Hugh Wilson, d 1/5/1966.

14   Eilen, wife of John Grawfurd, Sandyford, Co Dublin, d 19/12/1931 ? age 42yrs ?. John Grawfurd, d 22/6/1939 age 60yrs.

15   My husband, John JM Dowzer, Capt. RAMC. JP. LRCP and SIDPH. of Fern Acre, Eccles, Lancs, d 7/8/1932 age 64yrs.

16   James Pankhurst Knowles, d 1/7/1944 age 76yrs. His wife Charlotte, d 11/12/1959 age 94yrs. Daughter Charlotte, d 29/11/1982, youngest daughter Sarah Ellen, d 14/1/1992.

17 Anne Mary Sutton, daughter of John and Florence Sutton, Bridge House, Kilternan, d 26/7/1946. The above Florence Sutton, d 2/9/1949, her husband John Sutton, d 31/10/1952 age 85yrs.

18 Violet, widow of Arthur Marrable, Druid Hill, Cabinteely, d 15/9/1946.

19 William Richard (Jerry) Willis, d 27/8/1954. His wife Harriet Staple Willis, d 5/5/1958. Olive Willis, d 21/6/1971, her husband Eric Branscome Willis, d 14/7/1974.

20 Elizabeth Willis, d 18/9/1968. William Patrick Willis, d 14/4/1993. Parents of Lindy, Peter and Stephen.

21 T J Robinson, d 12/4/1950 age 67yrs, his wife Ethel Maud, d 20/9/1957 age 74yrs.

22 Our parents Joseph Walker, d 19/8/1953. Mary Louisa Walker, d 22/12/1959 of Fernhill, Sandyford, Co Dublin. Their grandchildren Andrew Philip Walker, d 16/3/1952 at birth and Rosemary Heather Walker, d 17/2/1953 ? age 12yrs. Philip Robinson Walker 1915-1982 of Balgara.

23 Our aunt Hester Ann Walker, d 11/5/1955. Norman Cornwall Walker of Annacreevy 1909-1980. Ralph Joseph Walker 1913-1980 of Fernhill.

24 My husband Samuel Cleary, d 3/12/1960. My brother Capt JW Hopkins, d 2/7/1954. Rebecca Mary Cleary, wife of Samuel, d 8/9/1965.

25 Topping - my husband Hubert (JHW), d 10/12/1989.

26 Sara Winifred DePauley 1891-1947. William Cecil DePauley 1893-1968, bishop of Cashel 1958-1968.

27 Arthur Henry Stevens, late RAF, son of William P and Gladys E Stevens, d 17/8/1945 age 20yrs.

28 Charles ???ard, d 28/5/1918 ? age 59yrs.

29 George Dowzer Hayes (GiGi), only child of William J Hayes LRCP.+ SE. and Nina his wife of Patricroft, Lancashire died in Dublin, Sunday 9/10/1921 age 20yrs. Dr. WJ Hayes, d 13/5/1956 age 91yrs. Nina Hayes, d 13/5/1955 age 76yrs. (plaque on grave) - A token of respect in memory of George Hayes from members of the British Legion, Eccles Branch.

30 My husband, Frederick John Somers, d 11/9/1942 age 39yrs.

31 William Brittain Mackay MD., d 15/2/1927, his wife Zaida Robina, d 20/3/1936. Frances E Smith, d 11/8/1925.

32 Evelyn Margaret Tracey, wife of Stephen Tracey, Ballyedmonduff, Sandyford, d 31/5/1932 age 23yrs. Stephen Tracey, d 28/12/1977.

33 Tracey - Loftus 1907-1972, his wife Sheila 1908-1999. Their daughter Margaret 1933-1934.

34 The Rev William Ralph Westropp Roberts, fellow of Trinity College, Dublin. DD., sometime Vice Provost of Trinity College, d 30/6/1935. His wife Lydia Mary, youngest daughter of George Hodder of Fountainstown, Co Cork, d 4/4/1933.

35 Dorothy Maud Conner, wife of Lt Col DG Conner, Mangh, Ballineen, Co Cork and eldest daughter of Dr. Westropp Roberts DD. SFTCD., Kelston, Stillorgan, Co Dublin, d 17/8/1938 age 53yrs.

36 Lil, d 11/7/1931. Lydia Mary Rogers, youngest daughter of John Wallis of Donnycarney, Co Dublin and for 25yrs wife of Charles Gilbert Rogers.

37 George Rothwell Harrison, d 10/1/1936 age 22yrs. Francis Richard Harrison, d 22/6/1944 age 25yrs. William Harrison, d 20/10/1955 age 88yrs. Elizabeth Anne Harrison, d 3/1/1958 age 75yrs. Edith Elizabeth Harrison, d 20/1/1973 age 61yrs.

38 Robert Millner, Gortmore, Eglinton Rd, Dublin, died May 1943, his wife Anna Maria, d 8/7/1963.

39 Kathleen Elizabeth Nelson, widow of Arthur Nelson of Armagh, d 10/1/1961.

40 Elizabeth Greany, widow of Thomas Greany, Muckrose, Millarney, b 15/8/1855, d 19/3/1935. Their daughter Elizabeth, b 13/8/1888, d 10/11/1988. Hilda Spencer Sheill, d 20/4/1952.

41 William Quinlan, 2nd son of the late Mr Justice Murphy, b 17/9/1873, d 24/2/1933.

42 Frances McIlroy, d 31/3/1931.

43 Sophia Violet Barrett VAD., St John's Ambulance Brigade, younger daughter of Samuel Barrett JP., of Ballintava, Co Galway, whose four years war service closed 10/10/1918 when returning to duty in France on RMC. Leinster torpedoed off the Irish Coast.

44 Marcella Anne Esther Wilson, 2nd wife of William H Wilson of Carrickmines House, d 3/8/1926 age 74yrs.

45 Mary Ann, wife of Arthur Marrable, Druid Hill, Cabinteely, d 12/2/1918. Their daughter Constance Irene, d 7/11/1940 age 55yrs. The above Arthur Marrable, d 13/5/1944 age 90yrs.

46 Edward Willis, b 5/8/1844, d 30/9/1919, his wife Annie, d 7/6/1939 age 93yrs. Son-in-law John Dick, d 3/9/1939 age 59yrs, his wife Anne Jane (nee Willis), d 31/7/1975 age 95yrs.

47 Tom Willis, d 14/8/1955 ?, his wife Annie Georgina, d 7/3/1981 ? age 94yrs ?.

48 Keeley - John James 1901-1903. Ellen 1903-1921. Mary Anne 1885-1929. Jane 1915-1929. Thomas 1879-1939. William 1915-1975. Thomas 1908-1990. Phyllis 1916-1995.

49 Mary Willis, d 5/5/1954. Marico Tomlinson, d 17/10/1951. William Armstrong Willis, d 11/11/1927.

50 William Bellingham Dobbs, Lisaivis, Dundrum, d 22/12/1927 age 60yrs, his wife Florence May Dobbs, d 12/3/1950 age 75yrs.

51 George William Ferguson, d 1/5/1928, his wife Arabella, d 1/6/1951. Samuel Joseph Willis, d 7/8/1968, his wife Kathleen Elizabeth (nee Ferguson), d 3/2/1987.

52 John William Large, d 16/6/1941 age 68yrs, his son Sydney George, d 5/3/1930 age 20yrs, his wife Letitia Alice Large, d 15/3/1959 age 78yrs. Albert Desmond Large, d 21/2/1989.

53 Katherine Anna Byrn, d 28/5/1962 age 85yrs, her husband Francis Ernest Byrn, d 24/8/1970 age 93yrs, formerly Cannon of Christchurch Cathedral and rector of this Parish for 29yrs. Their son Colonel Francis Macdermot Byrn, late RAMC, d 6/7/1985 age 72yrs.

54 Erected by Margaret Hatchell ilm her child George E Hatchell, d 24/1/1905 age 6yrs.

55 Francis Chaloner Smith, b 5/7/1858, d 16/6/1909.

56 John Brenan Esq, Kingston Lodge, d 2/8/1865 age 77yrs, his wife Emily, d 4/12/1841 age 41yrs.

57 John Griffith, his wife Sarah, daughter Florence and son John.

58 Francis Hendy, d 15/12/1921 age 80yrs.

59 John Sutton, d 20/9/1918 age 76yrs, his wife Catherine Sutton of Ballycorus House, d 4/5/1922 age 68yrs. Erected by their children.

60 1st stone - Sidney ER Fishbourne, daughter of Joseph Fishbourne of Ashfield Hall, Ballickmoyler, Queen's Co, d 10/8/1922 age 66yrs. 2nd stone - Annie Katherine Fishbourne died at Liskilleen, Shankill 31/9/1930.

61 Deborah Lavelle, d 2/4/1924 age 84yrs.

62   Louis Bewley, Blencarn, Foxrock died at Folkestone 7/12/1938 age 58yrs, his
      wife Charlotte Gilbborn Bewley, d 22/2/1965 age 85yrs.

63   Erected by William and John Hicks ilm their aunt Elizabeth Hicks, d 1/11/1903
      age 52yrs. Their sister Sissie Hicks, d 31/5/1915 age 36yrs. The above John
      Hicks, d 10/8/1916 age 26yrs.

64   James Dowzer, d 14/3/1898 age 69yrs, his wife Julia Sophia, d 22/3/1930 age
      84yrs.

65   Isabella Irvine, d 16/9/1909 age 85yrs.

66   Elizabeth Harding, d 20/9/1918 age 54yrs.

67   Samuel Jolley, d 10/3/1919. Gertrude Jolley, d 20/6/1958. William V Jolley,
      d 29/9/1969. Gertrude M Storey, d 27/12/1969. Percival R Storey, d 4/6/1970.

68   Helen Mary Kelly, elder daughter of John William Kelly, St Helens, Westport,
      d 4/11/1924.

69   Erected by Robert and Gracie Roberts ilm of their children, William Hamilton,
      d 20/7/1901 age 7yrs and Madeline Mary, d 3/1/1917 age 25yrs. Gracie
      Dowrick, wife and mother, d 21/1/1930 age 64yrs. Robert Roberts, d 6/7/1939
      age 85yrs.

70   Thomas F Sutton, d 21/5/1937 age 65yrs. Baby Eddie, d 30/4/1903.

71   Hannah Keegan, d 16/1/1894 age 58yrs.
72   My sisters Kathleen, Martha and Elizabeth Sutton who died in January 1925.
      Louisa Sutton, d 20/7/1906. Marian Sutton, d 19/6/1918. Sarah Sutton,
      d 29/12/1936.

73   Elizabth, wife of William Irvine QC., Prospect Hill, Carrickmines, d 7/2/1895.
      The above William Irvine KC., d 12/1/1913. Anne Catherine Frances, 2nd wife of
      William Irvine, d 29/11/1920.

74   Erected by Robert Taylor, ilm his father William Taylor, d 10/1/1885 age 75yrs.
      His mother Margaret 1802-1894. The above Robert Taylor 1839-1912, his wife
      Margaret Loftus 1837-1913. Their daughter Lucy E Agar 1872-1921 and son
      Robert 1880-1958.

75   Stone - Charlotte Sarah Strong, b 4/9/1820, d 2/10/1886. Flat Slab - Florence
      Elizabeth Mary, b 26/10/1863 ?, d 8/9/1866, daughter of Francis Henry Massey
      Sitmell Esq of Bormoor Castle, Northumberland.

76   Dorothy E Carter, late of Davenport Pk, Stockport, Cheshire, d 27/6/1953
      age 53yrs.

77   Elizabeth Kathleen, wife of Jack Sutton, Waterside, Kiltiernan, d 11/3/1956.

78 Arthur Mac Murroch Murphy, The O'Morchoe, d 7/3/1918 age 83yrs, his wife Susan Elizabeth, d 23/4/1924 age 83yrs. Thomas Arthur Mac Murroch, The O'Morchoe, rector of this parish for 28yrs, d 18/11/1921 age 56yrs, his wife Anne, d 26/2/1958 age 86yrs. Their 2nd son Lt Col. Kenneth Gibbon O'Morchoe, d 22/12/1962 age 68yrs, their 2nd daughter Honor Gertrude, d 9/7/1973 age 74yrs. Their 1st daughter Dorothy, d 3/1/1980 age 82yrs, their 3rd daughter Kathleen, d 9/8/1995 age 93yrs.

79 Nathaniel Mathew Hone, d 29/11/1912 age 58yrs.

80 Andrew Neely, Johnstown, Kiltiernan, d 19/10/1907 age 84yrs. Hercules Watkins Davis, Harcourt St, Dublin, d 24/10/1908 age 24yrs. Isabella Mary Davis, d 11/2/1917. Mary Davis, 63 Harcourt St, Dublin, d 23/3/1918 age 67yrs.

81 Livingston Flanagan (Livy), Ballycorus, a husband, father and brother, died Christmas 1904 age 45yrs.

82 John McConnell, d 6/10/1936, his wife Jane, d 10/8/1940. Edgar McConnell (Teddy), d 1/7/1990, wife Mabel, d 23/1/1992.

83 Thomas Stevenson, died September 1928, his wife Florence, died March 1959.

84 Erected by his wife ifm of Samuel Sherwood, age 42yrs, d 5/7/1886.

85 Anthony W Dwyer, d 9/8/1884 age 14yrs.

86 Robert Megan, d 30/3/1883 age 20yrs.

87 James Sutton of Ballycorus, d 10/5/1884 age 80yrs, his wife Margaret, d 24/6/1884 age 75yrs. Emily Jane, d 1/2/1890.

88 Samuel L Stevenson of Glenamuck, d 8/8/1884 age 61yrs. His brethern and friends of the Orange Institution have erected this stone.

89 Robert Stevenson, d 6/9/1918 age 65yrs, his wife Katherine Amelia, d 16/12/1912 age 68yrs. Their children Thomas Edward Greene (Eddie), d 4/6/1902 age 16yrs and Samuel Robert Little (Bertie) interred at St Thomas Churchyard, Dugort, Achill, d 3/11/1918 age 34yrs. Isabella, wife of Isaac W Stevenson of Brides Glen, d 26/10/1941 age 55yrs. Isaac William Stevenson, d 5/11/1945 age 66yrs.

90 Sarah Jane Walker, b 7/6/1850, d 16/3/1934.

91 Robert James Cross, d 14/2/1944, his wife Ivy, d 27/3/1958.

92 Elizabeth Bishop, d 30/10/1880 age 52yrs. George Bishop, d 18/8/1895 age 66yrs.

93 Mary Anne, wife of Robert Jolley, d 11/1/1894 age 56yrs. His daughter Anna

Maria, d 14/4/1882 age 16yrs. The above Robert Jolley, d 16/4/1915 age 78yrs. Ann Jane Jolley, wife of Christopher, d 1/7/1953. Christopher Robert, son of above Mary Anne and Robert Jolley, d 24/11/1935 age 65yrs.

94   Erected by William Tracey ilm of his wife Margaret Tracey, d 21/1/1924 age 56yrs. Her children - Lucy, age 7mths died 1889. Arthur, age 5mths died 1891. Margaret, age 3mths died 1893. William, age 21yrs died 18/3/1910. The above William Tracey, d 3/4/1947 age 85yrs.

95   Dorothy Hill, d 10/2/1997.(wooden cross)

96   Eileen M Talbot, d 4/3/1995.

97   John Spencer Hudson, d 1/9/1988.

98   Joseph Reuben Fisher, Archdeacon of Meath, Rector of Dunboyne Union 1946-1979, d 28/12/1989 age 79yrs. His wife Mary Crighton Fisher, d 27/1/1994 age 90yrs.

99   Samuel Jolley, d 30/5/1904 age 27yrs, his son William R Jolley, d 13/2/1904 age 11mths. Erected by his wife.

100 Erected by George Tracey ilm his father Edward Tracey, d 16/6/1904 age 75yrs, his mother Margaret Tracey, d 19/1/1909 age 78yrs. His son Edward John Tracey, d 3/12/1911 age 9yrs. John Tracey, d 17/3/1919 age 15yrs. The above George Tracey, d 13/1/1942 age 72yrs, his wife Esther Anne Tracey, d 20/8/1942 age 73yrs.

101 Mary (Lal) Freeman, d 9/9/1990, her husband Lionel, d 14/5/1995.

102 Adam Dillon Jolley, d 5/11/1990. His grandfather Albert E Jolley, d 6/8/1996.

103 My husband, Robin S Savage, d 17/9/1989, his wife Maureen, d 8/8/1994.

104 Eric Patrick Sholedice 1923-1991, husband of Ruth, father of Ann Marie.

105 George Norman Pillow, d January 1988. His daughter Jennifer Lynn, d. February 1992.

106 Shelagh Pheifer (nee Richardson), 1929-1992.

107 Samuel George Sievewright, Ballybetagh, Kiltiernan, d 25/2/1993.

108 Charles Samuel Madden, 1915-1993, Lt. Col. 60th Rifles.

109 Garry Elmes, d 17/11/1994 age 33yrs, husband and father.

110 Cyril Frederick Myerscough, d 16/3/1985 age 78yrs, his wife Joy, d 18/1/1996 age 83yrs.

111 My husband Thomas Kennedy, d 30/5/1979 age 72yrs, his wife Lily Kennedy, d 25/10/1989 age 81yrs.

112 Our sisters, Lilith (Pink) Mabel Haslam, d 13/5/1977. Donah (Blue) Deidre Haslam, d 1/1/1985. Enda May Vanderkiste (nee Haslam), d 22/1/1995.

113 Joseph Pierce, d 15/1/1978 age 78yrs, his wife Georgina Alexandra, d 26/2/1978 age 76yrs.

114 My wife, Mildred M Knowles, d 25/6/1978. Her husband Sydney Knowles, d 14/8/1981.

115 David McCloy Watson, d 22/1/1980.

116 Maurice Horan, d 7/12/1980, his wife Betty, d 19/6/1987.

117 Charlotte Hannah Pilkington, d 23/3/1981.

118 Constance Jane Harris, d 8/4/1984, her husband Arthur Harold, d 25/3/1985.

119 Our parents, Audrey Elizabeth Gresty, d 29/4/1985. Stanley LD Gresty, d. 31/7/1996.

120 Edward William Felton, d 2/1/1987 age 80yrs, his wife Jessica Kathleen, d. 5/11/1996 age 84yrs.

121 Davidson - Fiona Rosemary, a much loved daughter, 30/10/1956-30/3/1988. Doris Winifred, mother and wife, d 4/3/1997.

122 Elizabeth F McKinstry (nee Tracey), d 28/9/1996.

123 H.E.P. Anderson, d 30/11/1984, his wife Evelyn Ethel (Eva), d 12/10/1988.

124 Hugh HM Townsend, d 27/1/1974.

125 My husband, Stephen T Tracey, d 2/6/1974, our daughter Evelyn, d 11/5/1978. Hannah G, wife of Stephen T Tracey, d 24/8/1980.

126 Janet Muir Phillips, d 29/8/1975, her sister Daisy E Fairweather, d 19/4/1984. Dr Jay Fleming, b 27/11/1914, d 29/5/1997.

127 Ottolene Keeley, wife and mother, d 18/11/1975.

128 Maisie Tracey, d 24/1/1976, her husband Henry Tracey, d 5/4/1983.

129 A husband and father, Edgar Ruttledge, Foxrock, d 6/4/1976, his wife Florence, d 21/9/1982.

130 My husband, Fred Howard, d 14/8/1976 age 72yrs, his wife Irene F (Rene), d 8/2/1993 age 85yrs.

131 Thomas W Franks, d 18/11/1941, his wife Erma I Franks, d 6/2/1977. Maureen L Franks, d 12/8/1984.

132 Nora Kathleen Tate, d 3/5/1997, her husband Norman Alexander, d 16/1/1985.

133 Wilfred Ernest Judge, 13/1/1903-30/5/1981. Doris Elizabeth Judge, 21/11/1907-2/3/1995.

134 Michael Hall. Captain, late Royal Scots Greys, 27/10/1917-10/5/1984.

135 Kenneth G Larkin, b 25/2/1928, d 18/2/1998. (wooden cross)

136 Harrison - Neil , husband and father, d 9/6/1984.

137 My husband, William George Bannan, d 15/12/1969.

138 Col. Nial C O'Morchoe, The O'Morchoe, d 26/2/1970, his wife Jessie, d 2/3/1987.

139 Thomas Grant Hanna, d 27/8/1970, his wife Ruby, d 23/8/1982.

140 Rear Admiral Kenneth HL Mackenzie CBE. , 29/10/1970, his wife Elizabeth Olwen Mackenzie, d 18/10/1996, daughter Fiona Jean Elizabeth, d 4/3/1996. Jael Elizabeth, d 29/6/1995.

141 Thomas C Sutton, 1897-1971, his wife Matilda (nee Tutty) 1901-1996.

142 Robert HB Oliver, d 3/8/1971 age 23yrs.

143 Gladys Elliott, wife of Lt. Col. O'Connell-Fitz-simon of Glencullen House, Co Dublin, d 30/9/1971 age 68yrs.

144 My wife, Isabella Tracey, d 1/11/1971 age 79yrs. George Ernest Tracey, d 29/11/1973 age 78yrs.

145 Annie Alcock, d 30/1/1972 age 72yrs. William Albert Alcock, d 23/2/1975. William Robert Copeland, d 15/10/1988.

146 Alexander Talbot, d 3/3/1972. Our mother Jean Talbot, d 27/7/1981.

147 Alan Keith Thomson, b 18/8/1918, d 7/2/1974, a beloved husband and father.

148 Marjorie Elizabeth Pringle, d 13/7/1998 age 93yrs, her husband Alfred Denis, d 22/8/1998 age 96yrs.

149 Ralph Alan Meyer, d 30/4/1967.

150 Ethel Mary Meyer, d 25/12/1965, her husband Samuel W Meyer, d 28/4/1970.

151 Edwin W Booth, d 26/8/1966 age 86yrs, his wife Edith (nee Overend),
d 3/1/1969 age 83yrs. Lionel O Booth, d 31/5/1997 age 83yrs.

152 The Rev. Cannon Thomas H Scanlon, d 22/10/1967, his wife Ada Mary,
d 14/5/1989.

153 Irene Carter, d 18/1/1966.

154 Sarah Tracey, d 12/11/1967 age 68yrs. William Arthur Tracey, d 16/6/1971 age
74yrs. John (Jack) Tracey, d 5/4/1996 age 68yrs.

155 My wife, Violet Stevenson, d 8/1/1968. Her husband Thomas (Tom),
18/12/1993.

156 Mary Patricia Fisher, d 26/6/1968, her husband John B Fisher, Rector of this
parish 1951-1983, d 31/3/1997.

157 George Edward Eldon, b 17/1/1886, d 25/7/1973, his wife Margaret, (nee
Scanlon), b 23/9/1885, d 22/9/1978.

158 A. Francis Dixon, d 15/1/1936. Margaret K Dixon, d 1/3/1949.

159 Randal Martin St George Manseragh, died at Liverpool 13/12/1932 age 73yrs,
5th son of Lt. Col. John Craven Manseragh, late RHA. And JP. for Co's Cork and
Tipperary, of Rocksavage, Castletownroche, Co Cork. Southcote Manseragh,
d 3/5/1935 age 77yrs, his wife Francis Manseragh, d 21/7/1945 age 79yrs.

160 Ethel Maude Allen, d 2/12/1929 age 31yrs.

161 Jane Ethel Delap of Priorsland died November 1928. Alfred Delap, d 3/10/1943.

162 Marjorie Simms, d 18/4/1928 age 4yrs, daughter of W.M. and May Calwell,
Rathgar House, Dublin. Mary Elizabeth Ida, d 10/3/1949, wife of W.M. Calwell,
Bushy Park Road, Dublin. William Maunsell Calwell, d 27/4/1967.

163 Georgina E Naylor, d 31/1/1931 age 76yrs.

164 John Mitchell Aimers, d 6/10/1949.

165 Marie Myerscough, d 16/7/1927. Fred S Myerscough, her husband,
d 26/9/1954.

166 William Joseph Nelson, d 13/8/1926 age 77yrs. His son Samuel Tyndall Nelson,
died of wounds at Etaples, France 18/9/1916. His wife Annie, 26/2/1931 age
87yrs.

167 Charles Wisdom Hely, d 31/12/1939 age 73yrs. Edith Mary Hely of Oakland, Rathgar, Dublin, wife of Charles Wisdom Hely, d 18/9/1944.

168 William F Molony, d 3/1/1938, his wife Alexandra, d 8/10/1972. (plaque)- William Arthur Alexander Molony 1918-1985.

169 Mary Frances Molony, daughter of George Molony RM., d 19/11/1929 ?.

170 Maria Josephine Rutherfoord, eldest daughter of Joseph Clarke Rutherfoord, b 10/8/1857, d 31/7/1918.

171 Anna Louisa Rutherfoord of Foxrock Lodge, widow of John F Rutherfoord, b 28/11/1842, d 6/4/1918. Her son Claud John Rutherfoord, d 16/1/1941. His wife Donah, 1891-1988.

172 Katharine, wife of Arthur W Rutherfoord, d 16/4/1916. The above AW Rutherfoord, d 19/10/1938, his 2nd wife Anchoretta Louise, d 26/12/1973.

173 Large plot- Joshua David Chaytor, d 4/7/1908 age 46yrs, his wife Lucy Sophie Chaytor, d 12/5/1946 age 79yrs. Mary Primrose Jellett (Diddles), born January 1904, died May 1986. Matthew Barrington Jellett, b 29/3/1861, d 29/12/1925, his wife Belinda Grainger Jellett, age 77yrs, d 9/4/1942. Grandson- Thomas Barrington Jellett, b 23/1/1932, d 19/7/1974. Phyllis Jellett (Bluebell), b 3/12/1902, d 10/8/11907.

174 Emily Charlotte Wilson, wife of William H Wilson of Carrickmines House, d 18/8/1914 age 61yrs. William Henry Wilson, d 10/2/1931 age 79yrs. October 7th 1936 their elder daughter Constance Mitchell, The Grey House, Carrickmines.

175 Mary Moore Hughes, daughter of Rev E Hughes DD., late rector of this parish, d 11/9/1915.

176 Russell George, child of Rev Thomas M and Mabel Patey, d 25/1/1919 age 5yrs.

177 Richard M Burgess, 1915-1996, Valerie P Burgess, 1927-1998.

178 Mary Jane Dormer, 1901-1990.

179 Desmond M Hudson, 1913-1995.

180 John Willoughby Brooks, 1907-1997.

181 David Pedlow, 1931-1999.

182 Michael Hudson, 1951-1999.

Loughlinstown

Loughlinstown

At the centre of the burial ground there is a large granite stone with the following inscription :-

St Columcille's Hospital 1841 - 1991. 150th Anniversary. This stone was dedicated by Sister Angelis, Matron of the hospital from 1974 - 1991, to the memory of all those interred here.

"The noble ones of other times sleep here, quiet be they voice they would not be disturbed. Pain and hunger gone, they feel not winters cold. The shepherd has them now, safe within his fold".

12th October 1991.

1 Mrs Cody, d 4/4/187?, age 30yrs.

2 John Paul Gleeson, d 21/6/1983.

3 Erected by the officers of the Rathdown Union in grateful memory of Robert Sharpe, d 30/10/1899, age 48yrs.

4 Mary Brophy, age 30yrs, d 12/1/1889. (stone broken).

5 Hariet Parnell, d 21/8/1877, age 43yrs also P. J. Parnell, age 3yrs. (stone broken).

6 Rev Edward W Burton, for 22yrs Chaplin of the Rathdown Union Workhouse, d 3/5/1890, age 77yrs.

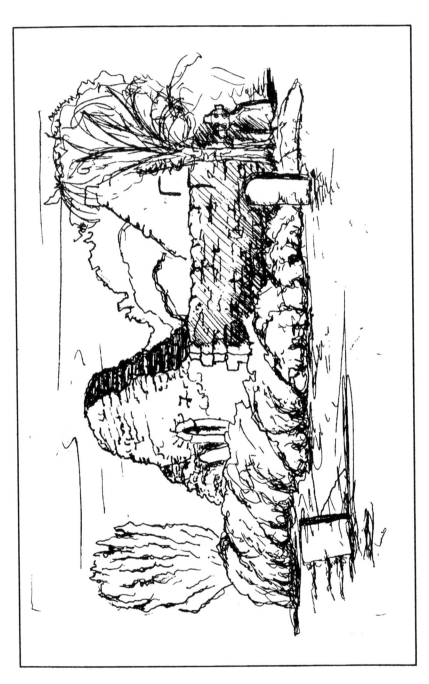

Old Connaught

Old Connaught

1 Erected by James Murphy of Dalkey ilm of his wife Isabella Murphy, d 28/1/1821 age 52yrs. His son James Murphy, d 6/7/1826 age 22yrs, his daughter Catherine Moore, d 4/9/1826 age 30yrs.

2 Erected by Thomas Healy of Kill O Grange, ilm of his wife Catherine Healy, d 16/12/1886 ? age 47yrs. William and John who died young. The above Thomas Healy, d 22/12/1914 age 75yrs.

3 Erected by Annie and Michael Skelton ilm their parents William Skelton, d 30/4/1913 age 62yrs and Catherine Mary Skelton, d 14/2/1921 age 62yrs. Their brother William Godfred, d 3/3/1919 age 27yrs. Here also lie the remains of their infant sister Kathleen and their grandparents Michael and Anne Toole.

4 WR/269250 Sapper W Skelton, Royal Engineers, d 3/3/1919 age 27yrs.

5 Hugh O'Neale, d 25/4/1719 age 56yrs.

6 Patrick Kenny, d 8/8/1817 ? age 79yrs, his wife Elizabeth Kenny, d 10/9/1809 ? age 62yrs.

7 Erected by his wife ilm of John Breen, d 30/5/1891 and is interred in Little Bray. Also their children who both died young.

8 George Walsh, d 20/12/1756 age 4yrs.

9 P Kavanagh served as 8/25292 Private P Ashford, Royal Inniskillin Fusiliers, d 1/3/1918 age 25yrs.

10 Three headstones, (stone 1) The Rev Luke White King LLD, died at Bray on 22/7/1873, his grandson George Lucas Stephen infant son of GH King MA, d 27/12/1873. (stone 2) Simon Christie, age 56 died 3/11/1795 ?, his daughter Margaret Hughes, age 33yrs, d 13/9/1799. His wife Mary, d 27/3/1800. Erected by Robert Christie of the town of Bray, son of Simon and Mary ilm of them, his sister and brother John, age 30yrs died 1799. (stone 3) Rev LW King LLD ex-sch TCD, born 23/3/1797 d, 22/7/1873. Mrs Hannah Christie who for upwards of 70yrs lived not for herself but for others and ceased from her labours May 5th MDCCCLIV. Erected by her children. Hannah Amelia, wife of Rev LW King LLD and daughter of Mrs Hannah Christie, d 23/7/1861 age 54yrs.

11 Erected by James Magee of Monkstown ilm of his wife Ellen, d 30/1/1884 age 26yrs. His grandfather Henry Magee, d 2/2/1877 age 80yrs. His daughter Mary Bridget, d 8/8/1887 age 7yrs, the above James Magee, d 5/4/1909 age 53yrs.

12 Erected by John Magee of Monkstown ilm his mother Mary, died November 1858, his father John Magee died February 1861. His daughter Mary, d 19/3/1877 age 12yrs and three of his children who died young. The above John Magee, d 14/1/1900 age 73yrs.

13 Henry John O'Toole, d 9/9/1872 age 22yrs, his sister Mary, age 16yrs (no date of death). Stone erected by their father Charles O'Toole of Shanganah AD 1873. His wife Margaret O'Toole, d 30/6/1880 age 65yrs.

14 Erected by John Murphy of Bray ilm of his sister Rosanna Sutton, d 28/4/1910 age 24yrs.

15 Erected by Patrick Dillon ilm of Con ? O'Neal of Bray, d 3/5/1812 age 61yrs ?.

16 Robert Clifton, d 24/10/1879 age 27yrs. Erected by his wife Mary Anne Clifton.

17 Mary wife of Ralph Jordan of Glendalough, died April 1860 age 37yrs, their daughter Kate died July 1857 age 9yrs.

18 Stone + burial place belongs to Ralph Jordan of the town of Bray. His daughter Catherine, d 4/5/1808 age 6mths. Elizabeth Jordan, d 6/6/1813 age 4yrs.

19 This stone and burial place belongs to Hugh Kelly of Old Court. Here lieth Barney Kelly, d 10/11/1814 age 31yrs, also Hugh, Margaret and Roseta Kelly.

20 Edmund William O'Kelly late of Bray in the county of Wicklow, d 4/4/1870 age 70yrs, his wife Mary Josephine O'Kelly, d 12/9/1871 age 64yrs.

21 Stone and burial place belongs to Mr Joseph Fitzpatrick of Bray. Here lie his son Joseph, d 7/7/1802 age 8mths, and his daughter Eliza, d 6/8/1807 age 4yrs. Their mother Elizabeth Fitzpatrick, d 7/5/1818 ?. Her husband Joseph Fitzpatrick, d 9/6/1833 ? age 65yrs. Michael Fitzpatrick his brother. Elizabeth Grehen, daughter of Joseph Fitzpatrick. Edmund William O'Kelly, d 6/4/1870 age 70yrs, son in law to the above Joseph and Elizabeth Fitzpatrick.

22 John Curran of Old Connaught, Bray, d 14/3/1882 age 52yrs, his brother Thomas Curran, d 15/12/1882 age 45yrs. John Henry O'Reilly (Jack), d 2/9/1885 age 6yrs. Katherine Harriett O'Reilly, d 19/2/1907 age 43yrs.

23 Erected by Bridget Mary Shortt, ilm her grandmother, Bridget Hackett, d 2/4/1879, her brother William Shortt, d 17/7/1885, her father John Shortt, d 20/9/1901, her sister Mary Walsh, d 5/5/1912.

24 Dudley Byrne, d 3/4/1829.

25 My husband John Gough, d 27/3/1913.

26 M Kennedy (no other information).

27 Bridget Cormick, d 17/3/1827.

28 Erected by Anne Butler ilm of her husband Charles Butler, d 3/1/1825 age 37yrs. The above Anne Butler, d 22/11/1837 age 52. Her grand daughter MA Daly who died young.

29 William Keating, d 26/2/1815 age 74yrs. John Keating, his brother d 10/6/1817 age 74yrs.

30 Erected by Thomas and Timothy Booth of Bray ilm of their father James Booth, d 9/11/1866 age 33yrs. Their grandmother Elizabeth Booth, d 12/8/1886 age

83yrs. Their brother James, d 22/6/1889 age 25yrs. Their mother Jane Booth, d 13/9/1891 age 58yrs. Their grandfather Thomas Booth, d 30/3/1892 age 82yrs.

31 William Flanagan, d 4/1/1878, Mary, d 4/5/1882 parents of Rev Joseph Flanagan PP. (St Margaret's and Finglas).

32 Thomas and Joseph Botts. Thomas, died 2nd of October and his brother Joseph on the 6th in the year 1822, Thomas aged 21yrs and Joseph 19yrs. Their father Thomas Botts, d 17/4/1829 age 55yrs ?, and his son Andrew ? (rest of stone sunk below ground level).

33 Erected by Margaret Cullen of Bray, ilm her father John Berney, d 8/4/1903 age 68yrs. Her mother Bridget Berney, d 10/11/1896 age 69yrs, her sister Catherine and her two brothers James and Peter who died young.

34 Erected by Pat Healy ilm of his father Pat Healy, d 11/1/1823 age 74yrs.

35 Erected by Matthew Lawless ilm his two sons Thomas and Matthew who died young.

36 Edward Leeson, d 17/2/1813 age 28yrs.

37 James Connor, d 11/7/1807 age 27yrs. Hugh Byrne, d 11/7/1807 age 35yrs also his two children. Patrick Murphy, d 13/11/1871 age 67yrs. Eliza Murphy, 18/6/1872 age 65yrs, both of Bray.

38 Robert Murphy, d 3/10/1931.

39 Erected by Elizabeth Lynch ilm of her husband Bernard Lynch, late Head Inspector of D.W.+WRLY, who was accidentally killed at Bray Railway Station on 27/12/1898 age 30yrs. Her children Bernard, d 12/12/1880 age 4yrs 3mths, Cecelia, d 5/11/1886 age 1yr 8mths. Mary and Patrick who died young. Anne, wife of Robert Lynch, d 23/6/1902 age 29yrs. Her daughter Agnes, d 12/4/1919 age 29yrs. Her sister Mary Mackie, d 25/9/1919 age 56yrs. The above Elizabeth Lynch, d 13/2/1927 age 78yrs.

40 Erected by Bridget Byrne ilm of her husband Christopher Byrne, d 22/6/1817 age 40yrs ?.

41 Erected by John Egan ilm of his daughter Mary, d 23/6/1890 age 13yrs.

42 Erected by Patrick Hall ilm his mother Mary Hall, d 20/11/1901 age 75yrs, his father John Hall, d 10/2/1907 age 84yrs. His wife Elizabeth Hall, d 11/3/1925 age 80yrs. The above Patrick Hall, 11/5/1930 age 84yrs.

43 Erected by Thomas Kenny of Bray ilm his mother Anne, d 2/9/1886 age 60yrs. His son Peter, who was drowned on 26/8/1899 age 9yrs.

Rathmichael

Rathmichael

1 Erected by William Trainor of Dalkey, ilm his son John, d 12/11/1899 age 15yrs, his daughter Mary, d 4/4/1901 age 21yrs. His wife Mary Anne Trainor, d 6/7/1902 age 50yrs and his son William, d 26/2/1903 age 15yrs.

2 Susan Rylands, d 13/8/1982.

3 Mary Kelleher. Jeremiah Kelleher. Norah Kelleher.

4 Erected by Daniel Carr of Dalkey ilm of his wife Catherine Carr, d 10/5/1846 age 36yrs.

5 The McNamara Family, Daleview, Ballybrack.

6 John Cunningham of Loughlinstown, d 18/2/1902 age 84yrs. His parents Patrick and Catherine Cunningham. His son Patrick who died young. His wife Hanorah Cunningham, d 9/10/1914 age 81yrs.

7 Dorah Lambe of 11 Castle Street, Dalkey, died December 1850. James, d 28/7/1861. Timothy, d 27/6/1868. Luke, d 5/5/1879.

8 Erected by Christopher Brady, ilm of his daughter Ann, d 13/9/1878 age 2yrs.

9 Patsy O'Halloran, 5/4/1941 - 29/7/1947.

10 Joanie, age 2yrs and her mother Kitty Kavanagh, d 29/4/1949, and her mother Mary Granny Thomas, d 31/10/1980 age 103yrs.

11 Mary C Butler, Cherrywood Road, d 21/1/1918 age 35yrs.

12 John Joseph Cunningham, d 2/3/1819.

13 Mary McCormack, d 11/3/1753 age 65yrs.

14 John, Mary and Michael Butler.

15 My husband, Patrick Clarke, 5 Library Rd, Shankill, d 9/8/1948 age 49yrs, his wife Jane (Gennie), d 23/4/1979 age 78yrs.

16 Hugh Denisson, d 1/2/1724 age 60yrs. Hugh Denisson died 1751. Joan Denisson, d 13/4/1754 age 89yrs.

17 John Higgins, d 17/2/1956 age 77yrs. His wife Ellen, d 13/2/1958 age 77yrs. (Stone broken).

18 Mary Byrne, d 20/9/1829 age 50yrs.

19 James Kelly, d 6/8/1821 age 27yrs, wife Anne Kelly, d 28/12/1843 age 49yrs.

20 Thomas Delaney, d 20/11/1942 age 51yrs. Sarah Delaney, d 8/5/1966 age 73yrs. Their son Stephen Delaney, died 1919 age 1yr.

21 Erected by Patrick Byrne of Shankill, ilm of his mother Bridget and two sisters Mary Murphy and Bridget Goff, 1898.

22 Erected by Esther Lambert ilm of her father Patrick Mason, d 18/2/1895 age 55yrs, her mother Catherine, d 10/2/1911. Her daughter Mary Lambert, d 10/1/1912 age 4yrs, her son Patrick, d 4/3/1912 age 7mths. Her husband Joseph Lambert, d 24/3/1952.

23 Maureen Leonard, d 11/2/1925. Thomas Leonard, d 23/8/1943. Teresa Leonard, d 9/12/1978.

24 My child, Patrick F Bell, d 1/12/1913 age 3weeks.

25 Edward McNally, d 6/1/1758 age 48yrs.

26 Our parents, Patrick McGarry, d 2/11/1944, Mary McGarry, d 5/9/1987.

27 Ann Dicken, d 10/6/1740 age 22yrs.

28 Erected by Elizabeth Farrell, ilm of her father Michael Farrell, d 13/1/1850 age 76yrs, her mother Bridget Farrell, d 31/3/1862 age 75yrs. Her brother Christopher, d 17/7/1878 age 62yrs. Julia Farrell, d 20/6/1875 age 60yrs. Elizabeth Farrell, d 1/7/1901, also Hugh and Bridget Farrell, d 13/7/1936.

29 Erected by Julia Cooper ilm of her husband Denis Cooper, d 17/8/1940, his mother Elizabeth Cooper, d 15/1/1941. Julia Cooper, d 30/9/1990 age 94yrs.

30 Erected by Myles Donnolly, ilm of his mother who died in 1862 and ?, also his child Julia, d 9/12/1870 age 3yrs.

31 ? Lee, died 1953, Annie Lee died 1947.

32 Erected by Mark Neil, ilm of his wife Mary, d 31/12/1868 age 56yrs, his daughter Letita, d 12/3/1852 age 9yrs. His mother Mary, d 8/3/1850 age 68yrs, his father John Neil, 3 ?/5/1850 age 70yrs and their other grandchildren who died young.

33 John Rylands, d 9/1/1959 age 80yrs. Mary Ann Rylands, d 22/4/1965 age 88yrs.

34 Catherine Mullen also Christopher Mullen and our dear mother Rose Kelly, d 17/9/1944, our father James Kelly, d 22/11/1948.

35 John Whelan, d 5/6/1981, husband of the late Elizabeth who died on 3/10/1957. Their son Desmond, d 20/1/1944.

36 ? Connolly, d 29/2/1922 age 8mths.

37 Christopher Reid, died in 1838, his wife Bridget died in 1858 also Patrick, John and Bridget sons and daughter of the above parents. This cross was erected by Christopher Reid, last surviving member of the above family and for 59yrs residing in South Africa 1906.

38 Erected by JJ O'Reilly of Temple Rd, Blackrock ilm of his father John O'Reilly, d 8/7/1897 age 66yrs, late of Cabinteely. His brothers Christopher, Patrick, George, Joseph and sister Margaret who died young. His mother Elizabeth O'Reilly, d 12/2/1900 age 60yrs.

39 Margret Graham, (sic) wife of Mr James Graham and her three children who died 7/7/1803 age 70yrs.

40 Michael Dixon, d 5/3/1921. Elizabeth Dixon, d 5/2/1935.

41 Alice Casey, Ballybrack, d 2/3/1913, her husband Patrick Casey, d 6/11/1918. Michael Casey, d 10/11/1958.

42 Thomas McGrath, d 3/9/1967 age 72yrs.

43 Erected by their family ilm of our father Andrew Waters, d 3/12/1933, our mother Ellen, d 20/2/1958, our sister Nellie, d 27/11/1958.

44 Our parents Patrick (Ted) Doyle, d 29/7/1950, his wife Hannah, d 15/11/1970, their son Michael, d 21/1/1982.

45 Esther Crosbie, d 13/3/1943 age 63yrs. Rose Brack.

46 Erected by Bessy Walker ilm of her husband Patrick Walker, d 6/12/1863 age 33yrs. Two of their children, George and Patrick who died young. His mother Catherine Walker, d 14/4/1854 age 77yrs, his father George Walker, d 1/4/1858 age 81yrs.

47 My daughter Philomena McGowan, d 6/3/1927 age 2yrs 10mths, my son Sean McGowan, d 26/6/1953, my husband Thomas McGowan, d 10/5/1957. Mary McGowan, d 29/8/1963. Ellie McGowan, d 9/1/1994.

48 Erected by Honor Donovan ilm of her parents John and Mary Donovan of Brennanstown, Co Dublin, d 1/2/1855 also their children Michael Donovan, d 30/10/1857 and Mrs Anne Monaghan, d 29/9/1871. Honor Donovan, d 25/8/1884. Catherine Magee, d 18/5/1909.

49 Jack Hopkins, d 11/3/1955 age 53yrs, his wife Sally Hopkins, d 13/12/1965 age 63yrs

50 Garreth Kelly, son of Michael and Mary Kelly of Montague Street, d 21/7/1808 age 16yrs, their daughter Mary age 8yrs. (no date of death).

51 Erected by Theresa Higgins of Loughlinstown ilm of her husband Patrick Higgins, d 14/3/1910 age 69yrs, his wife Theresa Higgins, d 14/4/1920 age 73yrs.

52 Susan (Sue) Smith, Shanganagh Vale, d 17/7/1994 age 57yrs.

53 Erected by Edward Waters ilm of his mother Bridget Waters, d 8/6/1934, his

father James who died in Huddersfield (no date of death), his brothers Andrew, d 27/2/1929, Arthur, d 25/3/1932. Julia Jackson (nee Waters), d 7/3/1946.

54 Erected by Catherine Cassidy ilm of her husband Joseph Cassidy, d 19/8/1909 age 58yrs. The above named Catherine Cassidy, died ?. (stone broken and embedded).

55 Our brother Robert Leonard, d 5/8/1941, our father Terence Leonard, d 30/6/1946, our mother Mary Leonard, d 30/10/1974.

56 Garrett Doyle, Bray Rd, Cabinteely, d 11/5/1943, his son Alexander, d 6/5/1957, his wife Anna Mary, d 24/11/1961. Anthony Doyle, 30/3/1948 - 9/4/1948.

57 Katherine Walsh, d 28/2/1914 and her son John age 3mths. Anne Bolton, d 18/2/1924 age 74yrs. Jacob Bolton, d 14/5/1924 age 84yrs. Mary Jane Bolton, d 31/5/1941 age 65yrs.

58 Our son, Daniel J O'Grady of Loughlinstown, Co Dublin, accidentally killed 5/10/1938 age 18yrs. His father William O'Grady, d 3/12/1941 age 58yrs. His mother Elizabeth, 29/12/1945 age 60yrs.

59 My wife, Bridget Bolton, Cherrywood Road, Loughlinstown, accidentally killed 5/3/1949. Her husband John Bolton, d 15/6/1950.

60 Erected by Patrick McManus ilm his daughter Eleanor, d 4/1/1888 age 2yrs 7mths.

61 James Murray, Castleknock, d 22/10/1929, his wife Jane, d 26/2/1959.

62 Our mother, Mrs Mary Casey of Mountain View, Ballybrack, d 18/10/1901 age 87yrs.

63 Julia Magee. Her husband Charles Magee. (no dates).

64 Winifred O'Brien, Monicas, Shanganagh, Shankill, d 2/2/1954, her husband Ed O'Brien, d 23/10/1918.

65 Michael Fleming of Ballybrack, d 5/1/1898 age 58yrs. His daughter Annie Teresa, d 10/11/1881 age 18mths. His wife Elizabeth, d 9/9/1916 age 75yrs, his daughter Elizabeth McBrien, d 12/6/1936, her husband Patrick McBrien, d 16/3/1956.

66 Erected by Patrick Doyle ilm his father John Doyle, Ballybrack, d 21/3/1929.

67 Erected by Bridget Byrne, Ballybrack ilm her father Garret Byrne, d 26/7/1876 age 89yrs, her mother Mary Byrne, d 22/8/1877 age 86yrs. Her brother Patrick Byrne, d 18/8/1818 ? age 10yrs?, her sister Mary Slacke ?, d 20/4/1895 age 60yrs.

68 My husband John Richmond, Galloping Green, Stillorgan, d 26/12/1942 age 44yrs.

69 Erected by Daniel Murray of Glasthule ilm his wife Margret (sic), d 7/5/1919 age 59yrs and their five children who died young. Daniel Murray, d 3/12/1936 age 87yrs.

70 Erected by Stephen Everard ilm his father William Everard, d 3/12/1877, his brother Thomas, d 1/3/1881, his two sisters Mary and Ellen. Christopher and Ann Everard.

71 Erected by Terence Kelly ilm of ????, d 20/9/1901 age 42yrs. His daughter Nannie ? died Jan 1892 age 3yrs.

72 Peter Kelly, 26/8/1885 - 8/11/1953.

73 Our parents Andrew and Mary Lee. Andrew was interred in the Seven Churches. Mary, d 3/6/1902 age 71yrs. Their two children, James who died young and Andrew, d 20/1/1907 age 45yrs. Katie, d 31/3/1918.

74 Patrick O'Rourke, d 10/1/1924. Julia Hickey, d 12/12/1926. Elizabeth O'Rourke, d 29/10/1934.

75 Sheila and Francis Gannon who died young.

76 Erected by William Maguire ilm his son William Maguire, d 16/11/1918 age 20yrs. His daughter Julia Maguire, d 20/2/1925 age 18yrs.

77 Mary Anne Lawless, d 21/10/1883 age 3yrs. James Lawless, d 21/9/1884 age 38yrs. Catherine Darcy, d 26/11/1906 age 58yrs.

78 Edward McDonald, d 9/4/1921. Sarah McDonald, d 30/8/1948.

79 Thomas Carter, d 5/11/1912, also his three children who died young.

80 William Lynch, d 10/9/1890 age 49yrs, his son Bernard, d 25/3/1892 age 30yrs. Daughter Mary, wife of Bernard Kelly, d 26/9/1893 age 30yrs.

81 My wife Mary Lynch, died May ???.

82 Thomas McNamee, d 14/10/1917, faithful servant of D Craig by whom this stone has been erected. His wife Elizabeth, d 26/7/1924.

83 My husband Robert Savage, d 30/10/1907 age 70yrs. His two sons David and Thomas. His wife Emily, d 10/9/1922 age 87yrs.

84 Our son Peter Richardson, d 18/2/1933 age 23yrs, his parents Julia Richardson, d 25/3/1965, and Peter Richardson, d 15/3/1966.

85 Ellen, wife of Richard Thompson, d 26/5/1881 age 36yrs. Their son John Henry, d 23/5/1875 age 2yrs 9mths.

86 William Hannan, d 20/11/1866, his wife Elizabeth, d 28/11/1889. The children of William and S Gilchrist, Freddy, d 16/11/1886, Alby, d 28/11/1886 and Ernest, d 26/4/1894.

87 Patrick "Paddy" Nolan, d 11/3/1951, his wife Mary "Mollie", d 26/5/1985.

St. Brigid's Church of Ireland

Saint Brigid's Church of Ireland

1 George Snow Murphy, 1900-1988, his wife Gladys nee Johnson, 1901-1990.

2 Michael Roy MacGregor, husband of Vyvian, d 30/10/1976.

3 Our darling Joanie. Joan Harriette Burgess SRN. 2/9/1934-16/5/1977.

4 Thomas S Hilliard, d 6/8/1985.

5 Walter Dunn, d 25/6/1991.

6 Douglas Jones, d 28/2/1981.

7 Ted Bannister, husband and father, 1918-1983.

8 Robert F Sharpe, Dec 1910- July 1986.

9 Sydney Giles, d 9/9/1976, his wife Violet, d 19/6/1998.

10 Albert Edward Gregory, d 5/7/1976.

11 Stephen R Booth, d 20/4/1978 age 27yrs.

12 Robert J Magill. D 15/1/1981.

13 Bentham Howe, d 27/4/1976.

14 Ruby Sarratt, 14/6/1907-26/6/1982. Her husband Alan Davenport Sarratt, 3/12/1905-25/1/1985.

15 Richard Edward Meates, 18/3/1900-19/11/1971.

16 Grace St. George Ormrod, of Lota, Foxrock, d 24/2/1973. Oliver Fray Ormrod, d 6/7/1978.

17 Eleanor Mary Preston, d 17/9/1975, her husband Benjamin Percival Preston, d 6/3/1982.

18 Ellen McQueston, d 11/3/1976.

19 Derrick Roy Craven, d 27/2/1974.

20 James Lindsay Crabbe, of Lissadell, Stillorgan, d 26/11/1970. Hilary, his wife, d 18/4/1986.

21 William LC Lindsay (Billie), b 3/3/1916, d 23/5/1971.

22   William Meates, d 10/7/1972, his wife Kathleen, d 26/8/1975.

23   Thomas Wardlaw, d 11/2/1974 age 78yrs, his wife Frances, d 8/1/1976 age 78yrs. Their daughter in law, Joyce Wardlaw, d 30/8/1984.

24   Henry Gardner, d 16/7/1967, his wife Emily, d 19/2/1978.

25   Margaret Webber Bateman, d 19/3/1968. Violet Bateman, d 10/11/1983, interred in Mount Jerome. Ernest Maunsell Bateman, Priest, d 8/4/1979.

26   Albert E Davidson, d 5/11/1969, his wife Bella, d 12/2/1971.

27   Kathleen Annie Walsh, 1911-1980.

28   Frances Shaw, Dec 1893-Nov 1969.

29   Leslie Scott McLusky, d 30/4/1971.

30   Robert Simmons, d 25/6/1971, his wife Elizabeth, d 11/7/1983.

31   John Theodore Francis Herrick, d 5/12/1965, his wife Charlotte, d 19/4/1966.

32   George Edward Greene, d 31/12/1965, his wife Jessie Amelia, d 19/2/1991.

33   Harold Vivian Mellon, d 8/1/1966 age 75yrs. His wife Bertha, d 17/12/1973 age 81yrs.

34   Dillon Henderson MacNamara, d 8/2/1967.

35   Gerald V Kuss, d 9/6/1969, his wife Alice, d 22/4/1996.

36   William Foot, 1889-1971., his wife Aileen Katherine Churling, 1893-1978.

37   Mary Mitchell, d 3/12/1964.

38   Our parents, Avery Gordon Palmer, 15/10/1873-21/3/1965. Co founder I.B.O.A. 1918. Active anti-vivisection movement. Charlotte Josephine Boyd.

39   William Hardinge Giffard Ryan, d 17/5/1965 age 57yrs.

40   Mona Evelyn Glanville, d 11/10/1965, her husband Eric Vance Glanville, d 29/10/1972.

41   Sarah E Trinder, d 7/7/1973.

42   Esme Frances Parkinson, d 27/8/1971.

43 My son, Tony. F.A. Rivaz, d 18/11/1952 age 35yrs. His mother Violet H Rivaz, d 18/12/1975.

44 Wm. G Hutchinson. MB., BCH. (Bill), d 20/1/1954 age 31yrs. Annie Ruth Hutchinson, mother of above, d 24/5/1975. John Hutchinson, husband and father, d 18/9/1976.

45 Alfred Rowland, 1875-1954, Elizabeth Rowland, 1877-1957, son Ronald, 1917-1987.

46 Sarah Elizabeth Hawkes, d 29/4/1954, her daughter Gladys, d 21/12/1979.

47 Juliet Rachel Boyd, wife of Rt Rev Robert M Neil Boyd, Bishop of Derry and Raphoe, d 29/1/1955.

48 Richard Medcalf, d 16/5/1955 age 75yrs. His wife Mary E (Jane), d 18/2/1973 age 85yrs. William H Medcalf, d 5/12/1965 age 88yrs, his wife Jane E , d 24/11/1970 age 89yrs.

49 A husband and father, William James Freeman, d 18/10/1967 age 81yrs. His wife Kathleen, d 3/9/1979 age 83yrs, their daughter Eileen, d 27/11/1980.

50 Arthur Herbert Stack Orpen of Brooklawn, Stradbrook, 3rd son of Arthur Herbert Orpen of Oriel, Stillorgan, b 27/7/1872, d 15/9/1953.

51 Dorothy Graham, d 31/5/1952 wife of Howard Graham.

52 Harry Thornton Hillas, d 16/3/1870 age 4yrs. Alice Hillas, d 13/5/1923. Francis Oliver Lyons, d 2/9/1935. Linda Hillas, d 21/6/1955.

53 Sarah Green, alias Tucker, 57yrs in the family of William S Magee Esq, of Parsons Green in this Parish. She was a faithful servant and humble friend, she departed this life trusting soley on the merits of her Lord and Saviour, Jesus Christ on 1/3/1846 age 93yrs.

54 Henry Guinness of Burton Hall, d 30/12/1893 age 64yrs. Emelina Guinness, his wife, d 4/10/1906 age 77yrs. Henry Seymour Guinness, their eldest son, d 4/4/1945 age 86yrs.

55 Robert Rundell, d 9/3/1857 age 67yrs. Mary Anne his wife, d 7/10/1889 age 76yrs. His 2nd daughter Susan Rachel, d 19/2/1892 age 48yrs. His daughter Edith Annie, d 19/5/1909 age 56yrs.

56 John Verschoyle, Esq, late of Stillorgan House in this Parish, d 27/6/1810 age 88yrs. Sarah Stuart, d 18/10/1846 age 76yrs.

57 Bryan Kavenagh, departed 46th year of his age in 1717. His wife Ann and their

son Edward. Their son in law, Thomas Ridgley, late of Blackrock who erected this stone to the memory of the above, he departed this life the 16/5/1786 age 78yrs.

58 Thomas Arthur, d 19/7/1867 age 18yrs. Henry Charles, d 12/7/1868 age 15yrs. Caroline Shortland, d 3/6/1858 age 1yr 7mths children of Henry and Caroline Maunsell. Thomasine, 4th daughter died in Dublin 20/2/1875 age 28yrs. Henry Maunsell, d 27/9/1879 age 77yrs. Constance, 2nd daughter, died at Dundrum 2/4/1886. Caroline Maunsell, d 2/3/1886 ? age 71yrs.

59 Edith Campbell, daughter of Captain H.A.M. Drought I.N. and Maria Helena his wife, b 19/7/1867, d 14/5/1875 age 5yrs 9mths. Mary Helena Drought, b 4/11/1864, d 30/12/1864. Blanche Mildred Drought, b 10/12/1868, d 13/11/1869. Captain H.A.M. Drought I.N., b 31/5/1814, d 4/3/1893. Maria Helena Drought, b 2/12/1831, d 22/10/1906.

60 Major J.R.H. Richards, late The Queen's Royal Regt, d 30/8/1931 age 82yrs. His wife Emily Anne Richards, d 16/3/1938 age 87yrs.

61 Mr. James Kearns of Nassau Street in the County of Dublin, d 14/4/1800 age 78yrs. Erected to his memory by his second wife Catherine Kearns.

62 David M Johnston, 1937-1998.

63 Gladys Regina Spoor, 1930-1996.

64 Judith Hutchinson, 1943-1995.

65 Esther Vincent, 2/3/1912-29/11/1994.

66 Lammie Wheeler, 1918-1984. Henry Aimers Wheeler, 1916-1993.

67 Douglas Victor Hutchinson, 1919-1992.

68 Harris.

69 John Edward Alfred Field, 1907-1992.

70 Margaret Scales, d 7/1/1995.

71 William Irwin Potts, 1923-1998. Iris Ann Potts, 1920-1998.

72 Capt Cecil Meredith, 1910-1989.

73 Richard Cecil Hughes, d 19/6/1994.

74 Eileen Morna Miller, 1905-1995. Alexandra Miller, 1903-1995.

75 Esther, wife of John Wickcliff Jones, d 6/5/1871 age 28yrs. Their only child Esther Allen Lole, d 3/11/1872 age 10mths. Anna Mary Byrne, daughter of John Jones, St Cloud, Kiltiernan, Co Dublin, d 1/3/1895 age 56yrs.

76 William Allebyrn, late of Stillorgan, d 10/5/1800 age 60yrs.

77 Florence Dora Louise Cornwall, daughter of Robert A Cornwall of Rutland Sq, Dublin, died at Burford, Clyde Rd, Dublin, 5/11/1931. Her brother Francis Victor Cornwall of Rathmore House, Naas, Co Kildare, d 22/12/1938.

78 William Ellison, late of Mount Merrion, d 9/8/1819. This stone was erected by John Kelly and Patrick Savage as a mark of friendship.

79 This stone and burial place belongs to Mr. Nich Ashe who has interred here his son William and daughter Martha. Also his son Joseph who died on 10/6/1781 age 27yrs.

80 Mary Elizabeth Darley, daughter of the late JH Darley, Ferney, Stillorgan, b 1889, d 24/5/1934.

81 Erected by Mr. James Graham of the City of Dublin imo his wife Mary Graham, d 7/7/1791 age 55yrs. Mrs Judith Cullen of Stillorgan, sister of the above Mary, d 9/4/1790 age 36yrs.

82 Mary Cooper, d 26/7/1953. Richard Cooper, d 28/7/1956. Violet Morrow, d 10/5/1960. Howard Morrow, d 5/8/1979.

83 Pamela Louisa Stanford, b 20/8/1821, d 1/2/1869. Pamela Charlotte Augusta, eldest daughter of Charles Stuart and Pamela Louisa Stanford, d 10/5/1868 age 23yrs.

84 Ernest Henry Lewis-Crosby, Dean of Christ Church Cathedral, Dublin and formerly rector of this parish, d 18/5/1961 age 96yrs son of Robert A Cornwall of Rathmore House, Naas. Hilda his wife, youngest daughter of John H Darley of Ferney, Stillorgan, d 27/11/1970 age 88yrs.

85 William Ladley, son of Thomas and Mary Ladley, died May 1856 age 17yrs. The above Thomas Ladley, d 20/7/1866 age 69yrs.

86 (Stone No.1) Blanche Georgina, infant daughter of Charles and Henrietta Wale of Shelford, Cambridgeshire, d 7/12/1859 age 7weeks. (Stone No.2) Blanche, wife of Capt C.H. Wale, RN. and youngest daughter of Richard Whately, Archbishop of Dublin, d 4/3/1860 age 30yrs.

87 Alice Clement, wife of P.C.F. Clement, d 7/11/1937. Percy C.F. Clement, d 10/2/1940. Their daughter Gladys, d 29/6/1978.

88 Erected by Daniel Magawly 20/April ?/1751. Here lies the body of Mary Magawly his daughter and the body of Judath Magawly his sister.

89 John S. MacIlwaine, died 1884. Rachel, his wife, died 1907. Their infant daughter Marian Cecilia, died 1863. Mary Elizabeth, daughter of John S. McIlwaine, died 1878.

90 Patrick McGuiness of the City of Dublin, d 21/1/1806 age 33yrs. This stone is erected by his widow Mary McGuiness. Allicia McGuiness, niece of the above mentioned Patrick, d 23/4/1809 age 20yrs.

91 Mary Catherine Morris, widow of John Morris, Rathpierce House, Inch, Co Wexford, d 10/7/1933 age 77yrs. Her son Lt. Col. Francis John Morris, M.C., T.D., R.A.M.C., d 12/10/1949 age 65yrs. Her daughter Elizabeth Morris, d 23/10/1957 age 74yrs.

92 Eleanor Harriet, wife of John Malam of the County of Norfolk, Esq and daughter of Henry Warner of Merrion Square Esq, d 14/10/1830 age 21yrs. Tomb erected by her husband 1830.

93 Peter Andrews Esq, late of the parish of Stillorgan, aged 56yrs, d 15/3/1811. Husband and Father.

94 Mary Elizabeth, age 6yrs. Caroline Frances, age 4yrs. Florence Isabel, age 2yrs. Robert Conway, age 5mths, children of Joshua W. and Hannah Egan, December 1874.

95 James Shea, late of Dublin, Joyner, d 25/1/1762 age 45yrs. To whose memory his wife Mary Shea ....(stone sunk below ground level).

96 William Brooke Esq, d 13/11/1825 age 86yrs. His son Henry Brooke Esq, late Major, H.M. 22nd Light Dragoons, died May 1833 ? age 34yrs ?.

97 Mary Jane, wife of William Johnston Johnston and daughter of Joseph and Martha Levingston of Avoca, Co Wicklow, d 17/11/1870 age 21yrs.

98 Mrs Mary Andrews, d 29/5/1848 age 82yrs. Erected by her only child Mrs Stewart.

99 Thomas Jackson of Farmleigh, Stillorgan, d 24/1/1936. Grace Mary, his wife, d 19/11/1944.

100 Thomas Jackson of Sunnyfield, Foxrock, d 6/6/1974.

101 (stone) Robert Smyth Esq of Cullenswood Ave, Co Dublin, died at an advanced age 12/12/1889. (slab) Frances Susanna Smyth daughter of Rob. Smyth of Leeson St, d 3/3/1809 age 8yrs 7mths. ?? Dickson, his mother in law and was

grandmother of the Rev Benjamin Dickson A.N.I. TCD., died March 1829 age 85yrs. Mary Smyth, his first wife, died May 1831 age 56yrs. Susanna Smyth, his 2nd daughter, d 27/8/1841 age 31yrs ?. Robert Smyth, Junior his son, d 30/3/1851 age 44yrs.

102 Mrs Mary Jones, wife of Mr. John Jones, d 29/10/1867. Her children Susan Hannah, d 21/6/1845, Susanah Amelia, d 24/11/1848, Sarah Maria, d 29/7/1856. Richard Lionel M.A., d 4/11/1879 husband and father. John 2nd son of the late James Jones of Tibradden Esq, d 30/11/1892 age 85yrs.

103 John Jolly, d 7/7/1878 age 81yrs. His wife Sarah, d 7/6/1887 age 52yrs. Their son Thomas, d 13/8/1872 age 19yrs. Their daughter Mary Jane, d 27/6/1890 age 21yrs. Sarah, d 30/4/1912 age 49yrs.

104 Mary Jane Jolly, d 15/4/1860 age 2yrs. Mary Margaret Jolly, d 18/11/1866 age 1yr. Their mother Mary Jane Jolly, d 20/10/1904 age 70yrs, their father John Jolly, 1/5/1905 age 84yrs.

105 Stearne Phillips Esq, d 27/9/1848. Joshua Phillips, Ashgreen, Co Meath, d 25/3/1861 age 41yrs. Annie his wife, daughter of the above, d 1/4/1903 age 76yrs. Their son Frederick William Phillips, d 13/6/1936 age 80yrs. His wife Frances Margaret, d 2/12/1951 age 92yrs. Their son Horace L. Phillips, d 14/3/1969 age 75yrs.

106 Ellen, wife of James Watts of Stillorgan Grove, d 27/9/1871 age 63yrs. Mr. J.S. Watts, husband of the above, d 6/4/1889 age 80yrs. A native of the town of Sligo. Their daughter Isabella. (no dates).

107 Douglas Haig Rath, 1917-1994. Sexton of this church 1951-1971.

108 Henry Browne Esq of Ballinvoher in the County of Cork, d 20/8/1849 age 73yrs. St John Edward, 3rd son of the above, b 3/3/1805, d 2/2/1880. Anna Constance, last surviving child of the above. (no dates). Henry Browne, b 9/2/1802, d 1/7/1881. Isabella, wife of the above St John Edward Browne, d 24/6/1904 age 84yrs.

109 Althea, 3rd daughter of Ford North Esq of Ambleside in the County of Westmoreland who died at Monkstown 15/2/1859 age 25yrs.

110 John Glynn of Stillorgan, d 1/10/1933, his wife Jane Glynn, d 22/5/1954.

111 The Rt Rev E.C. (Darby) Hodges 1887-1980. Principal of the Church of Ireland Training College Dublin 1928-1943. Bishop of Limerick, Ardfert and Aghadoe 1943-1960. Blanche his wife 1902-1966. Deidre their daughter 1933-1950.

112 Margaret only daughter of Richard and Margaret Massey, d 4/8/1862 age 16yrs. Her mother Margaret Massey, d 15/5/1867. Richard Massey, d 12/11/1888 age 73yrs.

113 My husband Hugh McHoul, d 9/6/1982, his wife Florence Elizabeth Harriet,
d 26/9/1995.

114 John Minchin Harkness, 1903-1982.

115 William Ivor Newman 16/1/1918-7/10/1980.

116 My husband Andrew Noel Newman, d 7/10/1964 age 77yrs, his wife Elizabeth,
d 7/10/1978.

117 My husband Claude Henry Fisk, d 31/8/1964, his wife Valerie, d 5/5/1973.

118 Frank Charles Thorp, d 19/8/1964, his wife Muriel Nicholson Thorp,
d 26/8/1964. His sister Dorothy Deacon, d 25/2/1972.

119 My husband William Herbert Mellon, d 24/6/1963.

120 Gertrude wife of Alick Buckley, d 7/6/1963. Alick Buckley, d 16/9/1983.

121 Timothy Bradford, Myrtle Lodge, Foxrock, d 22/2/1963 age 85yrs, his wife
Charlotte, d 11/2/1983.

122 Eric Carter Classon 1900-1975. Violet Classon 1900-1976.

123 Edwin Ernest Davis, d 21/11/1976.

124 William J Stringer, d 14/2/1977, his wife Louisa Margaret, d 27/2/1983.

125 Frederick George Ross MC., d 21/5/1979 age 82yrs, his wife Martha Kathleen,
24/9/1989 age 91yrs.

126 Canon Robert James Ross BD., 1909-1980. Precentor of Christ Church
Cathedral. His wife Mary Lydia, 1910-1994.

127 Thomas Alexander McDowell (Mac), d 6/4/1912.

128 Hugh Frederick Ouseley, only son of Frederick and Emmy Campbell,
b 21/5/1863, d 26/11/1863.

129 Edward McClelland Highton (Ned), d 29/9/1962 age 63yrs, his wife Eleanor
Annie (Nana) d 22/12/1979.

130 My husband John William Large (Jack), d 4/8/1962, his wife Alice, d 28/9/1982.

131 Robert W Carley, d 20/11/1994.

132 Maude Frances Annette Hart widow of George Vaughan Hart, Waltersland,
Stillorgan, b 27/1/1881, d 30/7/1961.

133 (stone 1.)Elizabeth Kidd died Whit Sunday 5/6/1960 age 91yrs, wife of the late
Samuel Kidd formerly of Limerick. (stone 2.) Thomas Hector Farnham
(Maurice) Bayly, 27/11/1902-18/1/1984, his wife Kathleen Elizabeth, daughter
of Samuel and Elizabeth Kidd, interred in Drumcondra 31/5/1906-2/2/1987.
Their daughter Helen Elizabeth 5/10/1932-18/2/1994.

134 Kenneth Arthur Charles (Ken) Goodridge RN. 1/6/1900-20/5/1958.

135 Major James Desmond Ward Harris (Jim), formerly RPC, born Bombay
30/5/1899 died Stillorgan 29/7/1958, his wife Mabel, born Dublin
28/3/1892 died 28/2/1960.

136 Edward Morgan, d 1/10/1958, wife Mary, d 17/6/1996.

137 A husband and father Derek Francis Digby Turpin, d 23/5/1983.

138 William Charles Henry Collins, born 1879 died 1961, wife Clara Louise Collins,
born 1877 died 1958 both of Leicester, England, son Clifford, husband of Anne
born 16/3/1909 died 11/11/1976.

139 (stone 1.) Derrick CA Cole, d 30/4/1978 age 60yrs, wife Iris, d 20/12/1995 age
74yrs.(stone 2.) Jonathan Cole, d 29/6/1959 age 76yrs, wife Flora, d 3/2/1976
age 89yrs.

140 My husband Gerald Walter Henry Walker, Rtd Major RHA. B 4/3/1892,
d 19/11/1959.

141 George Gordon Patterson 1911-1996.

142 Doris Finlater 27/4/1895-7/12/1981. ℓ Ol.

143 Daniel James, d 4/12/1859 age 5mths. John Dudley, d 29/1/1861 age 3mths.
Edith Mary, d 31/7/1867 age 4mths, the children of John and Susan Mills. Susan
Mills, age 44, d 27/12/1875. Alfred M Mills, age 17yrs, d 16/6/1880. John
Mills, age 53yrs, d 11/4/1884.

144 Herbert Edward Cecil Luggar, d 8/11/1974, wife Jessica Mary, d 8/9/1984.

145 Joseph Hastings, b 29/5/1883, d 6/4/1974.

146 Joseph Hume Dudgeon, Lt. Colonel Royal Scots Greys OBE. MC., Burton Hall,
19/3/1893-26/10/1965, wife I.F.M. (Sybil) Dudgeon (nee Symington),
b 9/6/1893, d 15/8/1975.

147 Louis Claude Fleury 1879-1957. Ethel Maude Fleury 1888-1972.

148 Stella Spencer, d 19/11/1997, her father Samuel Victor Spencer, d 11/2/1977, her mother Sara G Spencer, d 6/12/1979.

149 Richard Appleby, husband of Kathleen Appleby, Woodview Cottage, d 15/4/1959.

150 William Cambridge, d 10/5/1980.

151 The Rev HB Dobbs, late Precentor and Canon of St Patricks Cathedral, Dublin and 42yrs vicar of All Saints Church, Blackrock, d 14/2/1961 age 84yrs. Curate of Castlebar, Co Mayo 1902-1906. Curate of St Stephens, Dublin 1906-1914. His wife Kathleen, d 20/2/1982 age 101yrs.

152 Elizabeth Florence Sprengel, d 20/2/1958. Max Joseph Sprengel, d 19/11/1969.

153 Charles Cooper, d 23/1/1958. Ethel Cooper, d 11/10/1966. Ernest Cooper, d 27/11/1989.

154 Alexander Campbell (Monkey) Morgan late of the Royal Artillery, killed flying 18/1/1998 age 38yrs.

155 Mary Alice Skinner, d 28/11/1957 age 82yrs.

156 Our mother Alice Maude Downs, d 20/2/1955.

157 John Purnell Purnell-Edwards, formerly of Stancombe Park, Glougestershire, England, died at Stillorgan Rectory, 13/12/1956 age 70yrs.

158 Baby Elaine Dyer, d 3/7/1987.

159 My husband Edward Potter, d 7/6/1969, wife Eliza Jane, d 24/11/1988.

160 Charles McCarthy, d 8/8/1973 age 75yrs.

161 Francis Albert L'Estrange 1889-1976, husband of Eleanor, father of Rosemary. Eleanor Lucy Anne L'Estrange 1894-1983.

162 McCreedy - My husband Christopher, d 1/2/1974. Eileen his wife, d 20/2/1988.

163 Samuel Burton McCarthy, d 24/12/1979 age 76yrs.

164 Thekla Tune Beere 1901-1991, Civil Servant.

165 Ernest Gordon Costello, d 18/9/1973, wife Vera, d 24/1/1994.

166 George McAvoy, 27/8/1910-19/3/1983.

167 Isobella Henderson, d 10/5/1983. William James Agnew, 1928-1996.

168 Arthur McComas Johnson, b 1/1/1904, d 27/4/1956, wife Ethel Adrienne Johnson, 28/4/1905-19/9/1965.

169 Our mother Edith Alma Johnson, d 20/6/1956 age 81yrs.

170 John Allison, only son of Richard and Jean Large, d 13/5/1956 age 21yrs. Richard T Large, father of above, d 8/11/1985.

171 JHA Street, b 25/10/1881, d 17/4/1956. Mary his wife, d 19/5/1969.

172 Minnie Louise Thomas, d 8/7/1955. Arthur Rhys Thomas, b 29/3/1900, d 20/4/1978.

173 A husband and father George Spencer, d 12/6/1955 age 64yrs. Grandson Eric George Spencer, d 11/3/1963 age 9weeks, wife Emily Rose Spencer, d 18/2/1975 age 83yrs.

174 (Plaque on Garden Seat) Roger Beckett. Cub Scout Leader 1969-1991. 3rd Dublin. Stillorgan.

175 Hugh Burn, d 7/7/1722 age 55yrs.

176 Mary Minnitt, 3rd daughter of the late Joshua Minnitt Esq of Annaghbeg near Nenagh, Co Tipperary, d 24/1/1818 age 24yrs. Her mother Mary Toler Minnitt, d 21/10/1830 age 68yrs.

177 Henry Scovell, d 22/1/1861 age 70yrs, his wife Anna Maria, d 9/7/1875 age 77yrs. Charles Agustine Scovell, Gentleman Cadet of the Royal Military College, Sandhurst, d 16/11/1853 age 16yrs. His brother Fitzhenry Scovell, ensign HM 35th Regiment, d 2/4/1851 age 21yrs.

178 The burial ground of Henry Darley of Stillorgan. Here are interred the mortal remains of his mother Jane Darley, d 1/2/1806 age 68yrs, his brother Hill Darley, d 6/9/1807 age 33yrs. His father George Darley, d 21/8/1813 age 83yrs. Brother in law Richard Guinness, d 10/9/1929 age 74yrs. Mary, relict of Robert R Guinness, d 10/7/1837 age 33yrs. Mary, relict of George Hill, d 30/3/1846 age 54yrs. Cecilia Dixon, d 30/7/1849 age 24yrs. The above Henry Darley, d 22/11/1856 age 87yrs. His niece Frances, daughter of the above Richard Guinness, d 28/12/1888 age 96yrs.

179 Benjamin Clarke Esq formerly of Brides, in the City of Dublin, Merchant, d 4/8/1824 age 90. This stone was erected by his son Precious Clarke.

180 Anna Maria, wife of The Rev HYL Galbraith, rector of Rathdrum, d 24/12/1858. John Darley Galbraith, their only son, d 20/1/1867 age 8yrs 3mths.

181 Louise Antoinelle Pontet, age 64yrs, d 4/4/1834.

182 Anne Jane, wife of Isaac Barre Phipps of HM Council and Controller of Customs in the Colony of Berbice, d 29/6/1834 age 38yrs, her sister Elizabeth Mary wife of Michael Moloney Esq, d 7/8/1849 age 53yrs.

183 Baby Craig Thompson O'Doherty, d 20/1/1995.

184 Hilda Reid, d 23/4/1977.

185 Robert Medcalf, d 28/9/1835 age 10yrs, his father William Medcalf, d 1/3/1869 age 79yrs, his mother Catherine Medcalf, d 25/5/1877 age 84yrs. Their daughter Bessie, d 22/1/1880.

186 *Charlotte Isabella, eldest daughter of George and Charlotte Gough, b 29/11/1835, d ?/12/1854.

187 Alex MacLagan, b 12/1/1800, d 24/5/1855.

188 This stone and burial place belongs to Mrs Easterby of Williamstown. Here lies the remains of her grand children Mary Jane Burk, d 21/8/1823 age 5yrs. Eliza Burk, d 23/3/1830 age 11yrs.

189 Robert Vance, d 11/6/1810 age 63yrs ?.

190 Sarah Goff, wife of Joseph Goff, d 9/10/1803 ? age 37yrs. Joseph Goff, d 6/4/1855 ? age 79yrs.

191 Rev Edward Beatty formerly of this parish, d 21/3/1818. Humphrey Ffrench, brother in law of Rev Edward Beatty, d 7/1/1823 ?. Mrs Elizabeth Beatty, wife of Edward Beatty died June 1823 ? age 73yrs. Maria, wife of the above Humphrey Ffrench, (no date). Stone erected by Mrs Maria Ffrench.

192 Sarah, relict of Thomas Frederick St, Dublin, d 28/2/1856 age 79yrs.

193 *James Miller of Dublin, Attorney at Law, d 6/2/1763. His son Rev Oliver Miller, late of Prospect near Blackrock, d 14/4/1809 age 64yrs. John, Margaret and John Forbes, infant children of the Rev Oliver Miller. Rev James Vance Miller, eldest son of the above Oliver Miller, d 10/1/1818 age 45yrs. Henry Kyle Esq, late of Montpelier Parade near Blackrock who married Rebecca, eldest daughter of Oliver Miller died 19/1/1839 age 53yrs. Rebecca wife of Henry Kyle, d 21/1/1853. Charles Caulfield Atkinson, their infant grand son, d 7/5/1855. Charles Atkinson, d 8/5/1871. Rebecca Sarah, his wife d 7/10/1885, daughter of the above Henry Kyle.

194 Samuel Coombs, d 16/2/1851 age 37yrs, his mother Bridget Coombs, d 19/8/1853 age 80yrs. Eilen Coombs, d 2/2/1858 age 43yrs.

195 Rev George Knox, d 6/10/1874 age 71yrs. Frances Erskine Knox, his wife d 26/9/1886 age 75yrs.

196 Mary Edmonds, d 13/6/1862 age 36yrs, her mother Ellen Matilda Edmonds (nee White), d 18/11/1876 age 78yrs. The latter's sister Malvina Geoghegan, d 27/12/1893 age 80yrs.

197 Mary Nixon, eldest daughter of Montgomery Nixon Esq MD., formerly of Lakeview in Co Fermanagh, d 17/8/1854. Mary Nixon, 2nd daughter of Frederick T Nixon of Eden Lodge, Enniskillen, d 31/5/1895. Their nephew Alexander Edward Nixon, youngest son of Frederick Nixon of Eden Lodge of Fermanagh, d 25/6/1900. Elizabeth, eldest daughter of Frederick Nixon of Eden Lodge, Fermanagh, d 12/2/1902. Their eldest son Montgomery Nixon Esq BA. TCD., b 5/7/1848, d 7/9/1910.

198 This vault contains the remains of the under named members of the family of PA Leslie. His son Henry, d 16/2/1817 age 18yrs, daughter Jane, d 20/9/1820. Major Henry Leslie, d 13/10/1832. Charlotte Fleetwood, d 8/6/1834. Major Thomas Goodricke his son in law, d 19/4/1844. Sarah Anne Peacocke, his grandchild, d 16/1/1837. His daughter Sarah, relict of Major Peacocke, d 8/8/1851 ?. Charles Leslie, d 4/10/1879. His daughter Frances Leslie, d 13/5/1881 age 74yrs. His grand daughter Cath. W Peacocke eldest child of Goodricke and Arabella Peacocke, d 6/3/1871 age 10yrs. His great grandson Charles Leslie Wyndhan Peacocke youngest child of Peter Leslie and Iva Peacocke, d 24/6/1873 age 7mths. His great granddaughter Mary Leslie Peacocke eldest child of Peter and Iva Peacocke, d 22/7/1885 age 18yrs. Arabella Peacocke wife of Goodrike T Peacocke, d 20/3/1911. Goodricke Thomas Peacocke, husband of the above, d 15/10/1920. Frances Sarah Peacocke, daughter of the above, d 13/1/1929 age 66yrs. Ivaniona, wife of his grandson Peter Leslie Peacocke and daughter of the late Joliffe Tufnell, d 24/12/1901 age 55yrs. PA Leslie of Woodley in this Parish, d 1/11/1844 age 76. Sarah his wife, d 18/12/1847 age 76yrs.

199 Stone and burial place belongs to Thomas Uardon and ??(stone sunk).

200 Rev Robert Cage, rector of Rathconnell, Co Westmeath, d 12/9/1854 age 49yrs. Maria Cage his widow, d 2/12/1900.

201 A William Strean died July 1834 age 21yrs. Catherine Strean, his sister, d 8/6/1835 age 27yrs. Mary wife of Rev J Strean aged 40yrs, d 11/8/1853. His daughter Catherine Henrietta, d 23/6/1861 age 16yrs. His son Annesley William, d 30/6/1862 age 20yrs. His daughter Anna Maria, d 16/8/1866 age 27yrs.

202 Mrs Sophia Smyth, d 9/2/1831 age 69yrs.

203 Stone and burial place belongs to Patrick Coleman of the Podtle Merchant and his posterity. Here lies the body of the above Patrick Coleman, d 22/6/1764 age 57yrs.

204 John DeCourcy Hughes, eldest son of James Freeman and Martha Hughes, d 21/10/1874 age 24yrs. John Freeman Hughes Esq, of the Grove, Stillorgan,

d 29/12/1875 age 67yrs, his wife Martha, d 7/5/1896 age 83yrs.(stone worn)....
Mary Hughes ?, John Hughes ?.

205 (stone 1.) Anne Smyth, mother of Robert Smyth, AD 1795. Elizabeth Smyth,
wife of Robert Smyth, AD 1815. Their children, Robert, AD 1814, Bolton 1812,
George 1802, Sarah1806. (stone 2.) Erected by his wife in memory of Lt. Col.
RB Smyth, d 17/10/1888 age 61yrs.

206 Gina Agar, d 29/3/1999.

207 (stone 1.)George Drevar, late of the City of Dublin and also of Newtown in this
parish, d 17/8/1829 age 59yrs. Mary his wife, d 7/6/1845 age 65yrs. Mary his
eldest daughter, d 29/9/1867 age 69yrs. Harriette St Lawrence, his daughter in
law, d 13/6/1859 age 26yrs. (stone 2.) Elizabeth, d 21/7/1876. William,
d 5/4/1878. Emily DeCourcy, d 10/5/1884.

208 John Tubbs Esq, d 2/2/1804 age 56yrs.

209 Lieut. Henry Dawson, 9th Lancers, Drumartin Castle also his wife Letitia
(Stapleton) and their son William. This stone erected by their son Richard. Also
Rupert Vesey, Maximilian and Leonor Isabella, children of Major Richard
Dawson and his wife Jane and grandchildren of the above named Henry. Eustace,
age 23, son, grandson and brother of above, d 23/5/1884. Jane Luisa, wife of
Col. R Dawson 75th Regt., d 5/1/1887 age 54yrs, her son Raymond, d 8/3/1887
age 16yrs.

210 Mary Jane Winder, d 11/9/1873 age 60yrs. Williamina Deborah, 2nd daughter of
Edward Wm Winder Esq, d 11/11/1875 age 15yrs. Elizabeth Gervais Winder,
d 14/9/1939 age 81yrs. Mary Anne, wife of Edward W Winder, d 26/9/1912 age
82yrs.

211 Hic sepultus est Henricus Mason, Filius Gulielmi et Janae. Qui floris ritu
Gerininanus. Matutino golu depernt Anno Etat 7 Aug 18 1805. Edward W
Winder Esq, d 21/3/1880. His sister Alicia Barbara Winder, d 11/2/1894 age
92yrs.

212 Annie wife of William Mason of Newtown Pk, d 3/1/1860 age 55yrs. Their two
children Mary Annie and Henry Alfred Mason. The above William Mason,
d 14/7/1882 age 80yrs.

213 Craig Hamilton, b 22/11/1984, d 1/1/1999.

214 Esther Waldron, d 18/10/1871. Sarah, daughter of above, d 10/6/1869.

215 Henry Dawson Esq of Drummartin, Co Dublin, b 18/12/1781, d 12/1/18??. His
youngest son Rev William Augustus Dawson, b 19/4/1827, d 15/7/1857 ?, his
3rd son Henry Dawson Esq, b 25/6/1815 ?, d 30/9/1868. His 2nd son Rev Thomas

Dawson, b 3/1/1813, d 18/6/1872. His wife Emily Dawson, b 26/7/1788, d 4/3/1873.

216 Bryan Stapleton of the City of Dublin, d 23/7/1799 age 53yrs. Frances Stapleton his wife, d 27 ? /12/1808 age 57yrs. Mary Stapleton, daughter of said Bryan and Frances Stapleton, d 6/2/1806 ? age 20yrs.

217 In memory of the best of wives, mothers and sisters Elizabeth Meares, died 1792 age 47yrs.

218 *William Field, d 10/1/1799 age 7yrs. Thomas Jones Field, d 12/2/1803 age 14yrs, the children of William Hamilton Field Esq, formerly surgeon of HM frigate the Success and late of Blackrock in whose memory this is erected, he died 27/1/1832 ? age 75yrs. His widow and two surviving sons contemplated this tribute of respect to him. His younger brother William Jones Field AB. MB., died March 1843 ? age 34yrs ?. Rose Field, widow of the late William Hamilton Field, died aged 84yrs on 11/11/1845 leaving her son Henry Cary Field to deplore her loss. Jemima, wife of Henry Cary Field, Blackrock, Co Dublin, d 19/8/1851. Henry Cary Field MD, Blackrock, Co Dublin, aged 66yrs, d 11/1/1858.

219 Erected by William Poland ilm his father, mother, grandmother, aunt and sister Rosanna, also his brother Charles Eugene, d 26/12/1868 age 38yrs.

220 (stone 1.) Leonard Cornwell of the City of Dublin, d 9/6/1822 age 74yrs. John Cornwell of 36. Ruthland Sq, Dublin and Brownston House, Co Meath Esq, d 23/11/1862 age 73yrs. Dora his wife, d 15/5/1861 age 76yrs. Annie their daughter died August 1829 age 10yrs. Francis their son died July 1856 age 29yrs. Henrietta, their daughter, wife of Robert Cooke DL of Kiltinane Castle, Co Tipperary, d 13/6/1888 age 58yrs. John their son of Castlepark, Co Meath, d 24/3/1889 age 74yrs. (stone 2.) Robert Cornwell Lewis Crosby of Castlepark, Slane, Capt. Antrim Artillery, eldest son of Robert Cornwell of 36 Ruthland Sq, Dublin, b 9/10/1863, d 25/5/1890. Erected by his brother Francis Victor Cornwell. (stone 3.) Harriett Elizabeth Cornwell, widow of Robert A Cornwell Esq, d 26/10/1901 age 75yrs. Robert A Cornwell Esq, 36 Ruthland Sq, Dublin and Rathmore House, Naas, d 22/6/1892 age 64yrs. Erected by his widow.

221 Matilda Coates, relict of the late William Coates Esq of Killarney, d 14/5/1855 age 78yrs.

222 John Franklin Esq of Booterstown Ave in the Co of Dublin, d 18/3/1819 age 82yrs. Isabella, his wife died 27th of February in the same year age 73yrs. His 2nd daughter Elizabeth, d 10/6/1841 age 71yrs. Miss Susan Franklin, d 14/11/1849 age 39yrs. John Franklin, d 9/9/1837 age 84yrs. Mary Gamble, daughter of the above John Franklin and widow of Samuel Gamble of the City of Dublin, d 3/6/1871 age 89yrs.

223 Frances Elizabeth Beasley, d 3/11/1815 age 10mths.

224 Mary Doolan, d 24/2/1866 age 65yrs.

225 Samuel Jolly of Merville, Stillorgan, d 6/2/1898 age 65yrs. His son William, d 22/1/1872 age 6weeks.

226 Mrs Ann Bagley, wife of Mr Richard Bagley of Dublin, d 30/7/1787 age 40yrs

227 William Minchin Esq, of Eversham, Stillorgan, d 22/10/1843 age 49yrs. Erected by his widow Georgiana Minchin. Georgiana Minchin, his wife, d 28/4/1884 age 77yrs.

228 Erected by Mr William Weston, ilm of Letitia Weston, d 25/5/1768 age 16yrs.

229 Alice Mara, d 23/2/1757.

230 Rebecca, wife of William Cornwall of Richmond, Monkstown, Esq, d 8/3/1857 age 29yrs. Hastings Hennis, eldest son of William Cornwall Esq, d 20/7/1870 age 16yrs. Louisa Hennis, d 21/2/1877 age 90yrs. William G Cornwall Esq, d 13/10/1887. Marcella Rebecca, b 26/11/1893, d 30/12/1893 grand daughter of the above and daughter of Capt. Douglas William Cornwall and Emma his wife.

231*Erected by Mr Denis Council of Great Cuff Street for the use of him and his posterity. Here lies the body of Luke Council, d 1/7/1780 age 26yrs, and two of his children, Joseph and Mary Council.

232 Charles Cottell 1899-1986. Gwen Cottell 1904-1996.

233 Cynthia Joyce Skerritt 1921-1987. Albert Frederick James Skerritt 1918-1995.

234 Roy Hosgood, d 4/2/1988.

235 Eve Hollwey, Dunstaffnace, 18/7/1928-26/4/1988.

236 Terry Williamson, 1922-1990.

237 Ian Smeaton Couse, 1927-1990.

238 Jennifer Bryan, 22/1/1991 age 11days.

239 Ellen Gilchrist, 1903-1991.

240 Kenneth H Grove 1916-1990. Madeline F Grove, 1919-1991.

241 James Johnstone, d 3/9/1936.

242 Doreen Browning 1911-1991.

243 Leslie R Vaux 1913-1996. Jacki Troughton-Smith d 10/7/1986.

244 Canon Joseph Blackwell, d 4/1/1989. Heather Frances Calder, d 12/7/1984.

245 Sybil Margaret Shiell, nee Conyngham, d 8/3/1986. Major Roberet Derek Shiell, late York and Lancaster Regt., d 25/4/1989.

246 Syd T Ross 1911-1985. Doris Ross 1917-1996.

247 George Hunter Moffitt, d 17/9/1985.

248 Desmond Bradley, 1928-1985.

249 Walter Leonard 1914-1992.

250 Daddy- Frank Woodman, d 18/6/1973. Mammy- Aaltje Woodman, d 8/11/1985.

251 Sarah F Roulston 1903-1984.

252 Vera Colebrook, sister of Renne Smith, d 16/1/1984.

253 Henry Charles Cave MA, Canon of Christchurch Cathedral and rector of this parish, d 10/2/1947 age 70yrs.

254 Robert Ball, late vicar of Drumholm, in the diocese of Raphoe and chaplain of St Mathews, Ringsend who died near Stillorgan 12/5/1828 age 56yrs.

255 Frances Maria Viscountess Gough, b 9/8/1787, d 15/3/1863 ?. Hugh, 3rd Viscount Gough KCVO 1849-1919. Hugh William 4th Viscount Gough MC. 1892-1951. Field Marshal The Rt Hon Hugh 1st Viscount Gough, KPGCB. GCSI. KC. MS. PC., b 8/11/1779, d 2/3/1869. Jane Viscountess Gough, d 3/2/1892 age 76yrs. George 2nd Viscount Gough, b 18/1/1815, d 31/5/1895.

256 Henry, son of Henry Deane Grady Esq, d 3/12/1837 age 21yrs. William Deane Grady, d 12/1/1811. John Deane Grady, d Aug 1813. Standish Deane Grady, d 31/5/1816. Lady Muskerry, d 25/9/1816 and their mother,Dorcas Deane Grady, d 13/12/1857 relict of Henry Deane Grady of Stillorgan Castle and Lodge Co Limerick.

257 Edwin John Lloyd Webley, the only child of Daniel and Phoebe Webley, b 8/10/1859, d 4/3/1867.

258 Leonard Cornwall Jnr, eldest son of Leonard Cornwall of the City of Dublin, d 16/7/1800 age 21yrs. Leonard Cornwall Senr , d 19/6/1833 age 71yrs.

259 Laura, wife of John Burke Esq, and daughter of Adolphus Eugene Watson Esq. USN. ?, d 8/6/1866.

260 Humphrey Langley Handcock, d 9/1/1848 age 6yrs 8mths.

261 My mother, Caroline Louisa Elizabeth Ricketts, d 8/1/1949 age 89yrs. Lilian Frances Humphreys, d 15/3/1942, her sister Florence Eliza Humphreys, d 13/4/1951 age 88yrs.

262 *Jane widow of Capt. Raymond Tookey RN., late of Breaton Hill, Surry, died at Waltersland this parish 23/10/1814 ?.

263 Jane Amanda youngest daughter of William and Amanda Smyth of Waltersland, Stillorgan and niece of the above Jane Tookey, d 7/2/1845. William H Smyth Esq, died at Waltersland, 23/3/1850. Amanda Jane Smyth, wife of the above William H Smyth, d 3/6/1873 at an advanced age.

264 (stone 1.)Henry Rooke Esq, AM., d 8/5/1866 age 71yrs. Erected by his widow Elizabeth Rooke, who died 11/6/1886 age 82yrs. Their son William Duffield Rooke, d 23/10/ 18?? Age 31yrs. William Duffield Rooke Esq, d 6/12/1823 age 52yrs. Catherine Rooke his widow, d 7/12/18?3 age 85yrs. Eleanor E Rooke, daughter of Henry and Elizabeth Rooke, d 19/3/1883.

265 (stone 1.) Capt. Benjamin Warburton of HM Royal Navy, d 21/11/1828. Widow Elizabeth Warburton. Deborah Montgomery, daughter of DB and Eliz Warburton and relict of ?? Montgomery. (stone 2.)Capt. Barth Warburton, late of Birview in the Kings County. Resident magistrate for 37yrs, d 16/12/1860 age 75yrs. Anna Lucinda, his wife, d 8/1/1873 age 85yrs. Their only daughter Mildred Deborah Warburton, d 16/9/1910 age 85yrs.

266 Margaret, wife of Charles Doyne of Newtown Park Esq, the only child of her mother Harriet Doyne, she followed her into rest 31/5/1833.

267 Fanny Emily, wife of Rev Edward Groome, rector of Beaulieu, Co Louth, d 26/2/1845 age 43yrs.

268 Mary mother of George Chapman Esq of Castle Rheban, Co Kildare, d 2/8/1851 age 76yrs.

269 Deidre Leopold, d 1/7/1991 age 42yrs.

270 Reginald Christopher Peacocke MD. OBE., d 16/3/1936 age 65yrs, his wife Evelyn Clair Peacocke, d 31/10/1950?.

271 William Glynn, d 27/11/1965, his wife Ann Elizabeth (Lily), d 5/8/1993.

272 Jane Doran, d 8/3/1837 age 44yrs. Her infant daughter Eliza Jane age 10mths.

273 MacGregor Millar aged 3mths. Louis Ashworth Orr aged 5mths. Charles Louis Barrington Orr 13mths.

274 Erected by Mrs Mary Fitzharris of Galloping Green ilm of her husband Mr

James Fitzharris, d 30/10/1858 age 52yrs. Also his father, his sister Elizabeth and his son John.

275 Blanche Celestine, b 22/9/1879, d 12/5/1880. George Louis Alphonse, b 25/7/1878, d 27/10/1881, the two children of Alphonse and Lizzie Gages. Antoine, their 2nd son, b 28/6/1884, d 13/2/1885.

276 Charles Doyne Esq of Newtown Park, Co Dublin, d Wednesday 8/7/1857 age 82yrs. His widow Selina Helena Doyne, d 21/9/1868.

277 James Kennedy.(no date).

278 Jane, d 17/5/1822 ?, wife of John Gage Davis of Booterstown. John Gage Davis, d 6/6/1831 ?. Mrs Elizabeth Sarah Lyons, his sister, d 15/11/1846.

279 Arthur Phineas Murphy, d 9/4/1848 age 3mths.

280 Eliza Maria, wife of William Lyons, d 18/4/1888. The above William Lyons Esq, d 12/10/1889. George Irwin Scott, their grandson, d 5/12/1892 age 16yrs. Francis Moore Scott, father of above, d 28/4/1897 age 61yrs. Georgina Scott, widow of above, d 18/8/1927 age 91yrs. Theresa wife of John Charles Lyons and her infant son lie here 20/3/1821. Anne Tarbet, sister of the above Theresa, d 3/6/1834. John Tarbet, their brother, d 23/10/1836. John Charles Lyons, d 5/12/1869 age 87yrs. Mary Elinor Scott, d 8/8/1952 age 78yrs. Helena Violet Scott, d 11/12/1962 age 81yrs. Florence M Scott, d 19/8/1974 age 95yrs.

281 *Mary Griffith, widow of the late Richard Griffith, daughter of the late Chief Baron Burgh, d 8/9/1820 age 47yrs, three months after her husband. She was a tender mother.

282 Margaret daughter of the late Rev Francis Hall LLD, d 27/7/1843 ? age 49yrs.

283 *Sarah Harriett Hall, youngest daughter of Col. H Hall CB., d 1/3/1815 age 2yrs 8days.

284 *Richard Thwaites, d 19/1/1836. Elizabeth Thwaites, d 25/3/1882. Matilda Thwaites, d 18/9/1889 age 93yrs.

285 *Alexander Barrington Orr, d 14/12/1834 ? age 61yrs.

286 Ellen Thwaites, died Dec 1834 ? age 28yrs. John Thwaites, died May 1875 ? age 82yrs. Mark Bell Thwaites, d 22/9/7? age 74yrs. His 2nd wife Jane Thwaites, d. 25/9/1883.

287 Denise Andrews, 1920-1989.

Tully

Tully Graveyard

1   Edward Greene, d 21/10/1867 age 59yrs. His brother Thomas Green,
    d 25/11/1878 age 72yrs, Sarah, widow of Thomas Green, d 8/1/1886 age 75yrs.

2   Erected by James Brady of Castlepark Rd, Dalkey, ilm of his mother Esther
    Brady, d 1/6/1871 age 73yrs. His brother Stephen, d 25/8/1885 age 62yrs.

3   John Dillon, d 8/11/1791 age 66yrs, also his grandchildren John, Alice and
    Thomas Sherman.

4   A good wife and mother and a kind friend, the daughter of Capt Goddard of
    Newry, she was married to Samuel Greville of Carrickmines, Co Dublin, latterly
    of Rathgar. (no date given). Also Samuel Greville, husband of the above,
    d 2/12/1761 ? age 75yrs.

5   Erected by Mary Ball, alias Greville ilm of her husband Jonathan Ball,
    d 21/3/1795.

6   Erected by Patrick McGrath, ilm of his daughter Mary Dunne, d 1/5/1885 age
    32yrs. His son Joseph, d 14/4/1894 age 28yrs, also his two children who died
    young. His wife Esther McGrath, d 17/4/1896 age 61yrs.

7   Mr James Deeran, d 1/11/1811 age 40yrs.

8   Erected by John Robinson of Revan Street, ilm of his father and mother, Mrs
    Anthony Robinson, d 26/3/1760 age 47yrs and Mr Anthony Robinson,
    d 30/10/1766 age 61yrs and two of their daughters, Mrs Grey and Mrs Morgan.

9   Erected by Andrew Staunton of Patrick Street, Kingstown ilm of his father
    Patrick Staunton, d 15/12/1896 age 87yrs. Thomas Staunton, d 23/3/1895 age
    43yrs. Peter Staunton, d 29/9/1895 age 31yrs. Joseph, Maryanne, Christina and
    Honora Staunton who died at an early age.

10 Mrs Katherine Hutchisson, wife of Mr Joshua Hutchisson of the City of Dublin,
    d 14/9/1712 age 35yrs.

11 Geo Davis Sherry Esq of the City of Dublin, d 12/2/1794 age 45yrs, his wife
    Anne Sherry, d 28/12/1829 age 80yrs.

12 John Field, Main Street, Blackrock, d 9/6/1867 age 59yrs. His son John Joseph
    Field, d 31/7/1870 age 26yrs. Mary Jane, Frederick, Andrew, Francis and Patrick
    who died young. Edward Field, Dalkey, d 13/1/1889 age 31yrs. Grace Field, wife
    of John Field, d 21/1/1895 age 83yrs. Robert Field, 25/6/1908. Alfred Field,
    d 11/1/1910. Mary Field, d 22/12/1927 age 75yrs.

13 Erected by Mary Field of Cabinteely in the County of Dublin ilm of her husband
    Edward, d 8/8/1821 age 35 ? yrs and three children who died young. Their son
    Andrew, d 12/7/1873 age 52yrs, his wife Elizabeth, d 4/3/1863 age 42yrs and
    their children Robert, d 21/10/1874 age 21yrs, James, d 12/6/1885 age 33yrs,
    Edward, d 31/12/1885 age 42yrs, John, d 22/1/1900 age 54yrs. Also William
    Field, Donnybrook, d 30/11/1909 age 52yrs.

14 Erected by Augustine Grehan of Leaunstown ilm of his wife Anne Grehan,
    d 23/6/1841 age 36yrs. His daughter Margaret, d 8/6/1826 age 3mths. Mary his
    daughter, d 26/8/1849 age 22yrs. Augustine Grehan, d 10/11/1875 age 86yrs.
    His daughter Christina, d 13/5/1887 age 45yrs, his son James F Grehan,
    d 1/11/1896 age 60yrs. Lucy, wife of James, d 5/7/1901 age 63yrs.

15 Erected by James Reilly of Loughlinstown ilm of his son Patrick, d 13/5/1828
    age 1yr. His father in law Thomas Whelan, d 27/3/1820 age 60yrs. Mother in
    law Anne Whelan, d 22/9/1827 age 60yrs. His children Patrick and Mary who
    died young.

16 Erected by John Byrne of Cabinteely ilm of his wife Mary , 22/5/1880 age 60yrs.
    Also his infant son John. (no date of death).

17 Mary Hurley of Ballybrack, d 5/10/1911 age 23yrs. Her grand parents Frances
    Callaghan, d 15/2/1877 and William Callaghan, d 13/6/1896. Her sister Betty,
    d 6/9/1915 age 15yrs. Their mother Lizzie Hurley, d 28/11/1917, their father
    Christy Hurley, d 15/4/1931. Michael Callaghan of Cabinteely, d 26/7/1942 age
    72yrs. Erected by her parents.

18 William Byrne of 101 Lr, Georges Street, Kingstown, d 5/8/1902. His sons
    Michael, d 14/2/1891, John, d 22/2/1894, Christopher, d 3/12/1896 and
    William, d 20/4/1904.

19 Michael Byrne, d 18/6/1896, his wife Julia Byrne, d 3/8/1911 ?. Their son
    Michael, d 4/9/1927 ?.

20 William Clift of Carrickmines, d 2/1/1799, his daughter Fanny Clift died April
    1777.

21 Erected by Mr Michael Farrell, of Killiney, ilm of his father Mr Joseph Farrell,
    d 24/12/1837 age 102yrs. The above Michael Farrell, d 16/11/1866 age 60yrs.
    His mother, three sisters and two brothers are also buried here. His brother
    Benjamin Farrell, d 13/4/1884 age 80yrs. Elizabeth Farrell, wife of Benjamin,
    d 10/3/1886 age 74yrs.

22 Kate (nee McCahey), wife of G Rochford, died at Kingstown 5/3/1901 age
    41yrs.

23 Miss Mary Mercer, died June 1795 age 20yrs, second daughter of Patrick Mercer Esq by Ann his wife, both of Old Connaught in the county of Dublin.

24 Erected by James Moore, ilm his father Patrick Moore, died April 1849.

25 Nicholas Tannany ?, d 1/5/1756 ? age 70yrs. ? ? - only son.

26 Johnny Byrne, 1820 - 1910.

27 Erected by William Byrne, ilm of his mother Mary, d 15/7/1810 age 42yrs, his father John Byrne, died August 1828 age 70yrs.

28 Thomas and Maria Byrne, Glendruid, Cabinteely.

29 Lizie, daughter of Michael and Mary Shea, d 2/8/1879 age 20yrs.

30 Erected by Mary Boland, Kill of the Grange, ilm of her husband Nicholas Boland, d 22/1/1908 age 67yrs. His brother James, died 1856, his mother Emily Boland died October 1894.

31 Erected by Mary Fleming, ilm of her husband Michael, d 19/3/1871 age 84yrs, and one daughter who died young. The above Mary Fleming, d 13/11/1904 age 90yrs.

32 Erected by John Kirwan, Kill of the Grange, ilm of his father John, d 25/11/1831, his mother Mary, d 31/3/1876 age 96yrs. His wife Elizabeth, d 8/2/1870 age 51yrs. His brothers, Laurence, d 20/8/1836 age 17yrs, Daniel, d 14/4/1843 age 13yrs, James, d 11/10/1853 age ?, Thomas, d 13/3/1859 age ?, also two of his children who died young. Ellen Kinsella, wife of Denis Kinsella and daughter of the above, d 20/7/1878 age ?. Elizabeth, his daughter, d 23/7/1878 age ?. (headstone broken).

33 John Forsyth, his wife Margaret and their children.

34 Erected by John Ryan, ilm of his children, Bridget, d 6/8/1832 age 16yrs, Mary, d 4/5/1849 age 23yrs, and four of their brothers who died young. Celia aged 19yrs. Bridget Jun-15-, Catherine Jun 8-. Mary Ryan, wife of the above John Ryan, d 15/11/1867 age 66yrs. The above John Ryan, d 1/1/1885 age 86yrs.

35 Cecila Kearney, d 15/8/1854 age 41yrs. Four of her children who died young. Her father and mother, Patrick and Mary Rorke.

36 Erected by John Lambert, ilm his father, mother and brother Myles. His wife Kate Lambert, aged 41yrs, d 31/9/1898.

37 Patrick Connolly, d 4/1/1901 age 64yrs.

38 James Reynolds, d 4/11/1843 age 57yrs, his wife Mary, d 24/11/1854 age 68yrs. Christopher Reynolds, d 3/2/1907 age 86yrs.

39 Kathleen Fleming, d 6/9/1876, her husband Thomas Fleming, d 1/5/1881.

40 Erected by William and Margaret Doyle, ilm of their three children ?, ? and Therrese who died young. Also ? Kevans, d 27/11/1871 age 21yrs.

41 William Fitzpatrick of Cabinteely, d 8/2/1877 age 87yrs.

42 Erected by William Staunton, Cabinteely, ilm his mother Elizabeth Staunton, died February 1835 age 70yrs, and three of his children who died young. His son William Staunton, d 12/2/1868, his wife Mary Staunton, d 14/8/1869, his son James Staunton, d 31/1/1872, his son Thomas Staunton, d 20/2/1873. The above William Staunton, d 3/11/1884 age 86yrs.

43 Erected by her children, ilm of Mrs Anne Kelly of Glenageary, d 21/4/1886 age 67yrs, and her three children who died young. Their father Mr Thomas Kelly, d 17/2/1898.

44 Shusana Potts, d 12/9/1731 age 49yrs.

45 Erected by Richard Hall of Kingstown, ilm of his mother Hannah Hall, died 1865 age 85yrs. His wife Catherine, d 10/5/1877 age 60yrs, and infant child Anne. Michael, d 29/3/1879 age 26yrs. The above Richard Hall, d 23/10/1862 age 63yrs. His son Richard, d 29/12/1885 age 30yrs. His daughter Catherine, d 11/5/1893 age 30yrs. The above Richard Hall, d 23/10/1882 age 75yrs.

46 Erected by Thomas J Doyle of New York, ilm his father Richard Doyle, d 11/12/1868 age 44yrs, his mother Jane Doyle, d 28/2/1885 age 50yrs. His brother John Doyle, d 10/11/1867 age 24yrs.

47 Erected by Sarah Doyle, ilm of her husband Richard Doyle, d 20/7/1853 age 40yrs, also her three children who died young. Anne, her daughter, d 27/6/1883. The above Sarah Doyle, d 12/12/1885 ? age 73yrs.

48 William McCabe of Carrickmines, d 17/3/1810 age 74yrs. Daniel McCabe, d 9/3/1828 age 37yrs.

49 John Coyle, d ? age 67yrs. His sister Margaret Coyle, d 12/7/186? Age 22yrs. Margaret, wife of the above John Coyle, died November 1896 age 82yrs. (headstone broken)

50 This burial place belongs to the Walsh's of Carrickmines of the County of Dublin. William Walsh, d 20/6/1755 age 50yrs. Jane Walsh, his daughter, d 1/11/1755 age 25yrs.

Index of Inscriptions

NAME	DATES	LOCATION	Ref. No
??ARD	1918 ?.	KILTERNAN	28
AGAR	1999 .	ST BRIGIDS	206
AGAR	1921 .	KILTERNAN	74
AIMERS	1949 .	KILTERNAN	164
ALCOCK	1972, 75.	KILTERNAN	145
ALLEBYRN	1800 .	ST BRIGIDS	76
ALLEN	1929 .	KILTERNAN	160
ANDERSON	1984, 88.	KILTERNAN	123
ANDREWS	1848 .	ST BRIGIDS	98
ANDREWS	1989 .	ST BRIGIDS	287
ANDREWS	1811 .	ST BRIGIDS	93
APPLEBY	1959 .	ST BRIGIDS	149
ARCHER	1991 .	CONVENT	24
ASHE	1781 .	ST BRIGIDS	79
ASHFORD	1918 .	OLD CONNAUGHT	9
ATKINSON	1855, 71, 85.	ST BRIGIDS	193
BAGLEY	1787 .	ST BRIGIDS	226
BALL	1795.	TULLY	5
BALL	1828 .	ST BRIGIDS	254
BANNAN	1969 .	KILTERNAN	137
BANNISTER	1983 .	ST BRIGIDS	7
BARDON	1906 .	CONVENT	21
BARRETT	1918 .	KILTERNAN	43
BARRINGTON	1871 .	BARRINGTONS	29
BARRINGTON	1874 .	BARRINGTONS	18
BARRINGTON	1876 .	BARRINGTONS	42
BARRINGTON	1971 .	BARRINGTONS	41
BARRINGTON	1880 .	BARRINGTONS	40
BARRINGTON	1877 .	BARRINGTONS	39
BARRINGTON	1881 .	BARRINGTONS	37
BARRINGTON	1989 .	BARRINGTONS	36

BARRINGTON	1910 .	BARRINGTONS	35
BARRINGTON	1872 .	BARRINGTONS	33
BARRINGTON	1836 .	BARRINGTONS	43
BARRINGTON	1864, 70.	BARRINGTONS	12
BARRINGTON	1824, 69.	BARRINGTONS	1
BARRINGTON	1877 .	BARRINGTONS	2
BARRINGTON	1895 .	BARRINGTONS	3
BARRINGTON	1843 .	BARRINGTONS	4
BARRINGTON	1887, 1900.	BARRINGTONS	5
BARRINGTON	1901 .	BARRINGTONS	6
BARRINGTON	1942 .	BARRINGTONS	7
BARRINGTON	1915 .	BARRINGTONS	8
BARRINGTON	1902 .	BARRINGTONS	9
BARRINGTON	1913 .	BARRINGTONS	20
BARRINGTON	1893 .	BARRINGTONS	11
BARRINGTON	1890 .	BARRINGTONS	25
BARRINGTON	1847 .	BARRINGTONS	13
BARRINGTON	1917 .	BARRINGTONS	14
BARRINGTON	1893 .	BARRINGTONS	16
BARRINGTON	1828, 36.	BARRINGTONS	17
BARRINGTON	1877 .	BARRINGTONS	34
BARRINGTON	1906, 13.	BARRINGTONS	19
BARRINGTON	1915 .	BARRINGTONS	21
BARRINGTON	1928 .	BARRINGTONS	22
BARRINGTON	1928 .	BARRINGTONS	23
BARRINGTON	1925 .	BARRINGTONS	10
BARRINGTON	1834 ?.	ST BRIGIDS	285
BARRINGTON	1947 .	BARRINGTONS	32
BATEMAN	1968, 79, 83.	ST BRIGIDS	25
BAYLY	1984, 87, 94.	ST BRIGIDS	133
BEASLEY	1815 .	ST BRIGIDS	223
BEATTY	1818, 23 ?.	ST BRIGIDS	191
BECKETT	1991 ?.	ST BRIGIDS	174
BEERE	1991 .	ST BRIGIDS	164

BELL	1913 .	RATHMICHAEL	24
BENSON	1894 .	CONVENT	5
BERNEY	1896, 1903.	OLD CONNAUGHT	33
BEWLEY	1938, 65.	KILTERNAN	62
BISHOP	1880, 95.	KILTERNAN	92
BLACKWELL	1989 .	ST BRIGIDS	244
BLIGH	1868 .	CONVENT	12
BOLAND	1856, 94, 1908.	TULLY	30
BOLTON	1949, 50.	RATHMICHAEL	59
BOLTON	1924, 41.	RATHMICHAEL	57
BOOTH	1966, 69, 97.	KILTERNAN	151
BOOTH	1978 .	ST BRIGIDS	11
BOOTH	1866, 86, 89, 91, 92.	OLD CONNAUGHT	30
BOTTS	1822, 29, ?.	OLD CONNAUGHT	32
BOURKE	1946 .	CONVENT	27
BOURKE	1911 .	CONVENT	24
BOURKE	1895 .	CONVENT	4
BOWDEN	1944 .	CONVENT	9
BOYD	1955 .	ST BRIGIDS	47
BOYD	? .	ST BRIGIDS	38
BOYLAN	1861, 65, 77 ?, 79.	GLENCULLEN	36
BOYLAN	1925, 53, 56.	GLENCULLEN	92
BRACK	? .	RATHMICHAEL	45
BRADFORD	1963, 83.	ST BRIGIDS	121
BRADLEY	1985 .	ST BRIGIDS	248
BRADLEY	1883 .	CONVENT	8
BRADSHAW	1910 .	GLENCULLEN	139
BRADY	1871, 85.	TULLY	2
BRADY	1878 .	RATHMICHAEL	8
BRANNIGAN	1908 .	CONVENT	13
BREEN	1891 .	OLD CONNAUGHT	7
BRENAN	1841, 65.	KILTERNAN	56
BRENNAN	1948 .	CONVENT	24
BRENNAN	1959 .	CONVENT	6

77

BRENNAN	1996 .	CONVENT	9
BROOKE	1825, 33 ?.	ST BRIGIDS	96
BROOKS	1997 .	KILTERNAN	180
BROPHY	1889 .	LOUGHLINSTOWN	4
BROWNE	1849, 80, 81, 1904.	ST BRIGIDS	108
BROWNING	1991 .	ST BRIGIDS	242
BRYAN	1991 .	ST BRIGIDS	238
BUCKLEY	1963, 83.	ST BRIGIDS	120
BURGESS	1977 .	ST BRIGIDS	3
BURGESS	1996, 1998.	KILTERNAN	177
BURGESS	1910 .	CONVENT	23
BURGH	1820 .	ST BRIGIDS	281
BURK	1823, 30.	ST BRIGIDS	188
BURKE	1886 .	CONVENT	7
BURKE	1917 .	CONVENT	2
BURKE	1866 .	ST BRIGIDS	259
BURN	1722 .	ST BRIGIDS	175
BURTON	1890 .	LOUGHLINSTOWN	6
BUTLER	1825, 37.	OLD CONNAUGHT	28
BUTLER	? .	RATHMICHAEL	14
BUTLER	1918 .	RATHMICHAEL	11
BUTLER	1895, 1901, 02, 09, 16, 17.	GLENCULLEN	116
BUTTERLY	1922 .	CONVENT	27
BYRN	1962, 70, 85.	KILTERNAN	53
BYRNE	1924 .	GLENCULLEN	46
BYRNE	?,?.	GLENCULLEN	67
BYRNE	1872, 73, 80.	GLENCULLEN	39
BYRNE	1891, 94, 96, 1902, 04.	TULLY	18
BYRNE	1909, 10.	GLENCULLEN	127
BYRNE	1903, 09, 19, 49, 54, 63.	GLENCULLEN	107
BYRNE	1807 .	OLD CONNAUGHT	37
BYRNE	1832 .	GLENCULLEN	43
BYRNE	1926, 41.	GLENCULLEN	100
BYRNE	1853, 70, 73, 77.	GLENCULLEN	52

BYRNE	1829 .	RATHMICHAEL	18
BYRNE	1904, 17, 40.	GLENCULLEN	35
BYRNE	1896, 1911 ?, 1927 ?.	TULLY	19
BYRNE	1880.	TULLY	16
BYRNE	1915, 38.	GLENCULLEN	55
BYRNE	1910, 53.	GLENCULLEN	129
BYRNE	1829 .	OLD CONNAUGHT	24
BYRNE	1879, 90, 1903, 20, 46.	GLENCULLEN	95
BYRNE	1810, 1828.	TULLY	27
BYRNE	1817 .	OLD CONNAUGHT	40
BYRNE	?, ?.	TULLY	28
BYRNE	1925 .	BARRINGTONS	10
BYRNE	1898 .	RATHMICHAEL	21
BYRNE	1934 .	CONVENT	21
BYRNE	1895 .	ST BRIGIDS	75
BYRNE	1910.	TULLY	26
BYRNE	1818 ?, 76, 77, 95.	RATHMICHAEL	67
BYRNE	1854 .	CONVENT	14
CAGE	1854, 1900.	ST BRIGIDS	200
CAHILL	1932 .	CONVENT	2
CALDER	1984 .	ST BRIGIDS	244
CALLAGHAN	1877, 96, 1942.	TULLY	17
CALWELL	1928, 49, 67.	KILTERNAN	162
CAMBRIDGE	1980 .	ST BRIGIDS	150
CAMPBELL	? .	GLENCULLEN	37
CAMPBELL	1854, 64, 66.	GLENCULLEN	25
CAMPBELL	1863 .	ST BRIGIDS	128
CARLEY	1994 .	ST BRIGIDS	131
CARR	1846 .	RATHMICHAEL	4
CARROLL	1916 .	GLENCULLEN	44
CARROLL	1942, 46, 60, 71, 79.	GLENCULLEN	32
CARROLL	1929, 38.	GLENCULLEN	97
CARROLL	1924, 29, 51.	GLENCULLEN	86
CARTER	1953 .	KILTERNAN	76

CARTER	1966.	KILTERNAN	153
CARTER	1912.	RATHMICHAEL	79
CARTY	1932.	CONVENT	8
CASEY	1901.	RATHMICHAEL	62
CASEY	1913, 18, 58.	RATHMICHAEL	41
CASSIDY	1909.	RATHMICHAEL	54
CAULIN	1878.	GLENCULLEN	51
CAVE	1947.	ST BRIGIDS	253
CHAPMAN	1851.	ST BRIGIDS	268
CHAYTOR	1908, 46.	KILTERNAN	173
CHRISTIE	1795 ?, 99, 1800, 54, 61.	OLD CONNAUGHT	10
CHURLING	1978.	ST BRIGIDS	36
CLARKE	1858, 64.	GLENCULLEN	60
CLARKE	1948, 79.	RATHMICHAEL	15
CLARKE	1824.	ST BRIGIDS	179
CLASSON	1975, 76.	ST BRIGIDS	122
CLEARY	1954, 60, 65.	KILTERNAN	24
CLEMENT	1937, 40, 78.	ST BRIGIDS	87
CLIFT	1777, 99.	TULLY	20
CLIFTON	1879.	OLD CONNAUGHT	16
COATES	1855.	ST BRIGIDS	221
CODY	187?.	LOUGHLINSTOWN	1
COLE	1959, 76, 78, 95.	ST BRIGIDS	139
COLE	1938.	CONVENT	26
COLEBROOK	1984.	ST BRIGIDS	252
COLEMAN	1764.	ST BRIGIDS	203
COLGAN	1927.	CONVENT	17
COLLINS	1887.	CONVENT	23
COLLINS	1958, 61, 76.	ST BRIGIDS	138
CONNER	1938.	KILTERNAN	35
CONNERY	1985.	CONVENT	2
CONNOLLY	1922.	RATHMICHAEL	36
CONNOLLY	1901.	TULLY	37
CONNOR	1807.	OLD CONNAUGHT	37

CONNOR	1920.	GLENCULLEN	124
CONWAY	1876 .	GLENCULLEN	46
CONYNGHAM	1986 .	ST BRIGIDS	245
COOK	1901 .	CONVENT	15
COOKE	1888 .	ST BRIGIDS	220
COOMBS	1851, 53, 58.	ST BRIGIDS	194
COOPER	1953, 56.	ST BRIGIDS	82
COOPER	1958, 66, 89.	ST BRIGIDS	153
COOPER	1940, 41, 90.	RATHMICHAEL	29
COPELAND	1988 .	KILTERNAN	145
CORMICK	1827 .	OLD CONNAUGHT	27
CORNWALL	1931, 38.	ST BRIGIDS	77
CORNWALL	1800, 33.	ST BRIGIDS	258
CORNWALL	1857, 70, 77, 87, 93.	ST BRIGIDS	230
CORNWALL	1961, 70.	ST BRIGIDS	84
CORNWELL	1822, 29, 56, 61, 62, 88, 89.	ST BRIGIDS	220
CORNWELL	1890, 92, 1901.	ST BRIGIDS	220
COSTELLO	1973, 94.	ST BRIGIDS	165
COTTELL	1986, 96.	ST BRIGIDS	232
COUNCIL	1780 .	ST BRIGIDS	231
COYLE	186?, 1896.	TULLY	49
CRABBE	1970, 86.	ST BRIGIDS	20
CRAVEN	1974 .	ST BRIGIDS	19
CRONIN	1987 .	CONVENT	18
CROSBIE	1943 .	RATHMICHAEL	45
CROSBY	?.	GLENCULLEN	1
CROSS	1944, 58.	KILTERNAN	91
CULLEN	1790 .	ST BRIGIDS	81
CULLEN	1844, 66.	GLENCULLEN	28
CULLEN	1937 .	GLENCULLEN	18
CULLEN	1920, 46, 73.	GLENCULLEN	78
CUNNINGHAM	1902, 14.	RATHMICHAEL	6
CUNNINGHAM	1819 .	RATHMICHAEL	12
CURRAN	1882 .	OLD CONNAUGHT	22

81

DALY	? .	OLD CONNAUGHT	28
DALY	1937 .	CONVENT	28
DALY	1872, 92.	GLENCULLEN	14
DALY	1923, 46, 84.	GLENCULLEN	93
DALY	1877 .	GLENCULLEN	13
DARCY	1906 .	RATHMICHAEL	77
DARLEY	1934 .	ST BRIGIDS	80
DARLEY	1806, 07, 13, 56.	ST BRIGIDS	178
DARLEY	1970 .	ST BRIGIDS	84
DAVIDSON	1969, 71.	ST BRIGIDS	26
DAVIDSON	1988, 97.	KILTERNAN	121
DAVIS	1976 .	ST BRIGIDS	123
DAVIS	1822 ?, 31 ?.	ST BRIGIDS	278
DAVIS	1908, 17, 18.	KILTERNAN	80
DAVITT	1902 .	GLENCULLEN	106
DAWSON	1884, 87.	ST BRIGIDS	209
DAWSON	1818, 57 ?, 68, 72, 73.	ST BRIGIDS	215
DEACON	1972 .	ST BRIGIDS	118
DEANE	1913 .	BARRINGTONS	20
DEERAN	1811.	TULLY	7
DELANEY	1919, 42, 66.	RATHMICHAEL	20
DELAP	1928, 43.	KILTERNAN	161
DENISSON	1724, 51, 54.	RATHMICHAEL	16
DePAULEY	1947, 68.	KILTERNAN	26
DICK	1939, 75.	KILTERNAN	46
DICKEN	1740 .	RATHMICHAEL	27
DICKSON	1829 .	ST BRIGIDS	101
DILLON	1791.	TULLY	3
DIXON	1921, 35.	RATHMICHAEL	40
DIXON	1849 .	ST BRIGIDS	178
DIXON	1936, 49.	KILTERNAN	158
DOBBS	1927, 50.	KILTERNAN	50
DOBBS	1961, 82.	ST BRIGIDS	151
DOHERTY	1906 .	CONVENT	11

DOLAN	1920 .	GLENCULLEN	89
DONNOLLY	1862, 70.	RATHMICHAEL	30
DONNOLLY	1892, 1918, 27.	GLENCULLEN	63
DONOVAN	1855, 57, 71, 84.	RATHMICHAEL	48
DOOLAN	1866 .	ST BRIGIDS	224
DOOLEY	1910 .	CONVENT	7
DORAN	1837 .	ST BRIGIDS	272
DORMER	1990 .	KILTERNAN	178
DOWLEY	1906 .	CONVENT	10
DOWNS	1975, 78.	KILTERNAN	9
DOWNS	1955 .	ST BRIGIDS	156
DOWRICK	1930 .	KILTERNAN	69
DOWZER	1932 .	KILTERNAN	15
DOWZER	1898, 1930.	KILTERNAN	64
DOYLE	1958 ?.	GLENCULLEN	135
DOYLE	1926, 38 ?.	GLENCULLEN	90
DOYLE	?,?.	GLENCULLEN	12
DOYLE	1867, 68, 85.	TULLY	46
DOYLE	1950, 70, 82.	RATHMICHAEL	44
DOYLE	1850, 67, 69, 83.	GLENCULLEN	11
DOYLE	1943, 48, 57, 61.	RATHMICHAEL	56
DOYLE	1902, 06 ?, 07, 17.	GLENCULLEN	104
DOYLE	1853, 83, 85?.	TULLY	47
DOYLE	1868 .	GLENCULLEN	121
DOYLE	1929 .	RATHMICHAEL	66
DOYLE	?,?.	TULLY	40
DOYNE	1857, 68.	ST BRIGIDS	276
DOYNE	1833 .	ST BRIGIDS	266
DREVAR	1829, 45, 59, 67, 76, 78, 84.	ST BRIGIDS	207
DROUGHT	1864, 69, 75, 93, 1906.	ST BRIGIDS	59
DUDGEON	1965, 75.	ST BRIGIDS	146
DUNN	1991 .	ST BRIGIDS	5
DUNNE	1881 .	GLENCULLEN	134
DUNNE	1885.	TULLY	6

DWYER	1884 .	KILTERNAN	85
DWYER	?,?.	GLENCULLEN	1
DYER	1987 .	ST BRIGIDS	158
EAST	1950, 51, 91.	KILTERNAN	6
EASTERBY	?.	ST BRIGIDS	188
EBENRECHT	1914 .	BLACKROCK	4
EDMONDS	1862, 76.	ST BRIGIDS	196
EDWARDS	1956 .	ST BRIGIDS	157
EGAN	1890 .	OLD CONNAUGHT	41
EGAN	1874 .	ST BRIGIDS	94
ELDON	1973, 78.	KILTERNAN	157
ELLIOTT	1971 .	KILTERNAN	143
ELLIS	1946 .	GLENCULLEN	79
ELLISON	1819 .	ST BRIGIDS	78
ELMES	1994 .	KILTERNAN	109
EVERARD	1877, 81.	RATHMICHAEL	70
FAGAN	1882 .	GLENCULLEN	46
FAIRWEATHER	1984 .	KILTERNAN	126
FARRELL	1837, 66, 84, 86.	TULLY	21
FARRELL	1850, 62, 75, 78, 1901, 36.	RATHMICHAEL	28
FARRELL	1903 .	CONVENT	18
FARRELL	1933 .	GLENCULLEN	61
FARRELL	1855 .	GLENCULLEN	38
FELTON	1987, 96.	KILTERNAN	120
FERGUSON	1928, 51, 87.	KILTERNAN	51
FFENNELL	1917 .	BARRINGTONS	14
FFENNELL	1882 .	BARRINGTONS	15
FFRENCH	1823 ?.	ST BRIGIDS	191
FIELD	1867, 70, 89, 95.	TULLY	12
FIELD	1908, 10, 27.	TULLY	12
FIELD	1821, 63, 73, 74, 85.	TULLY	13
FIELD	1900, 09.	TULLY	13
FIELD	1830 .	GLENCULLEN	133
FIELD	1799, 1803, 32 ?, 43 ?.	ST BRIGIDS	218

FIELD	1845, 51,58.	ST BRIGIDS	218
FIELD	1992 .	ST BRIGIDS	69
FINLATER	1981 .	ST BRIGIDS	142
FISHBOURNE	1922, 30.	KILTERNAN	60
FISHER	1989, 94.	KILTERNAN	98
FISHER	1968, 97.	KILTERNAN	156
FISK	1964, 73.	ST BRIGIDS	117
FITZACHARY	1828, 38, 1900, 03.	GLENCULLEN	27
FITZACHARY	1899, 1928.	GLENCULLEN	26
FITZHARRIS	1858 .	ST BRIGIDS	274
FITZPATRICK	1802, 07, 18 ?, 33 ?.	OLD CONNAUGHT	21
FITZPATRICK	1877.	TULLY	41
FITZSIMON	1865, 99, 1937.	GLENCULLEN	9
FLANAGAN	1878, 82.	OLD CONNAUGHT	31
FLANAGAN	1915, 30.	GLENCULLEN	57
FLANAGAN	1904 .	KILTERNAN	81
FLEETWOOD	1834 .	ST BRIGIDS	198
FLEMING	1881, 98, 1916, 36.	RATHMICHAEL	65
FLEMING	1997 .	KILTERNAN	126
FLEMING	1876, 1881.	TULLY	39
FLEMING	1898 .	GLENCULLEN	134
FLEMING	1871, 1904.	TULLY	31
FLEURY	1957, 72.	ST BRIGIDS	147
FLOOD	1898, 1904, 05.	GLENCULLEN	3
FLOOD	1898 .	GLENCULLEN	101
FLYNN	1967 .	CONVENT	26
FOLEY	1854 .	CONVENT	18
FOLEY	1943 .	CONVENT	20
FOOT	1971, 78.	ST BRIGIDS	36
FORRESTER	1911 .	CONVENT	5
FORRESTER	1880 .	CONVENT	9
FORSYTH	?,?.	TULLY	33
FOX	1907, 11, 26, 30, 39.	GLENCULLEN	130
FRANKLIN	1819, 37, 41, 49, 71.	ST BRIGIDS	222

85

FRANKS	1941, 77, 84.	KILTERNAN	131
FREEMAN	1967, 79, 80.	ST BRIGIDS	49
FREEMAN	1990, 95.	KILTERNAN	101
FRENCH	1950, 71, 81, 92.	KILTERNAN	7
GAGES	1880, 81, 85.	ST BRIGIDS	275
GALBRAITH	1858, 67.	ST BRIGIDS	180
GALLAGHER	1969 .	CONVENT	5
GALLAGHER	1923, 39, 76.	GLENCULLEN	72
GALLAGHER	1843 .	GLENCULLEN	24
GAMBLE	1876 .	BARRINGTONS	42
GAMBLE	1871 .	ST BRIGIDS	222
GANNON	? .	RATHMICHAEL	75
GARDNER	1967, 78.	ST BRIGIDS	24
GASKIN	1926 .	GLENCULLEN	20
GEOGHAN	? .	CONVENT	19
GEOGHEGAN	1893 .	ST BRIGIDS	196
GILCHRIST	1991 .	ST BRIGIDS	239
GILCHRIST	1886, 94.	RATHMICHAEL	86
GILES	1976, 98.	ST BRIGIDS	9
GILMARTIN	1937 .	CONVENT	23
GLANVILLE	1965, 72.	ST BRIGIDS	40
GLEESON	1983 .	LOUGHLINSTOWN	2
GLYNN	1894 .	GLENCULLEN	101
GLYNN	1933, 54.	ST BRIGIDS	110
GLYNN	1965, 93.	ST BRIGIDS	271
GODDARD	?.	TULLY	4
GOFF	1803 ?, 55 ?.	ST BRIGIDS	190
GOFF	? , 1898.	RATHMICHAEL	21
GOODRIDGE	1958 .	ST BRIGIDS	134
GOUGH	1809, 63, 92, 1919, 51.	ST BRIGIDS	255
GOUGH	1854 .	ST BRIGIDS	186
GOUGH	1913 .	OLD CONNAUGHT	25
GOWRAN	1899 .	CONVENT	3
GOWRAN	1857 .	CONVENT	13

GRADY	1811, 13, 16, 37, 57.	ST BRIGIDS	256
GRAHAM	1952 .	ST BRIGIDS	51
GRAHAM	1803 .	RATHMICHAEL	39
GRAHAM	1791 .	ST BRIGIDS	81
GRAWFURD	1931 ?, 39.	KILTERNAN	14
GREANY	1935, 88.	KILTERNAN	40
GREAVES	1832, 40, 44.	GLENCULLEN	23
GREEN	1846 .	ST BRIGIDS	53
GREENE	1867, 78, 86.	TULLY	1
GREENE	1965, 91.	ST BRIGIDS	32
GREGORY	1976 .	ST BRIGIDS	10
GREHAN	1826, 41, 49, 75, 87.	TULLY	14
GREHAN	1896, 1901.	TULLY	14
GREHEN	? .	OLD CONNAUGHT	21
GRESTY	1985, 96.	KILTERNAN	119
GREVILLE	1761 ?.	TULLY	4
GREVILLE	?.	TULLY	5
GREY	?.	TULLY	8
GRIFFITH	? .	KILTERNAN	57
GRIFFITH	1820 .	ST BRIGIDS	281
GRIMES	1993 .	CONVENT	14
GROOME	1845 .	ST BRIGIDS	267
GROVE	1990, 91.	ST BRIGIDS	240
GUILFORD	1953, 66.	KILTERNAN	3
GUINNESS	1893, 1906, 45.	ST BRIGIDS	54
GUINNESS	1829, 37, 88.	ST BRIGIDS	178
HACKETT	1879 .	OLD CONNAUGHT	23
HACKETT	1942, 63.	GLENCULLEN	59
HALL	1843 ?.	ST BRIGIDS	282
HALL	1862, 65, 77, 79, 82, 85, 93.	TULLY	45
HALL	1845 .	ST BRIGIDS	283
HALL	1984 .	KILTERNAN	134
HALL	1901, 07, 25, 30.	OLD CONNAUGHT	42
HAMILTON	1999 .	ST BRIGIDS	213

HAMMOND	1910 .	CONVENT	9
HANDCOCK	1848 .	ST BRIGIDS	260
HANNA	1970, 82.	KILTERNAN	139
HANNAN	1866, 89.	RATHMICHAEL	86
HARDING	1916, 19.	KILTERNAN	1
HARDING	1918 .	KILTERNAN	66
HARKNESS	1982 .	ST BRIGIDS	114
HARRIS	1984, 85.	KILTERNAN	118
HARRIS	? .	ST BRIGIDS	68
HARRIS	1958, 60.	ST BRIGIDS	135
HARRISON	1984 .	KILTERNAN	136
HARRISON	1936, 44, 55, 58, 73.	KILTERNAN	37
HART	1961 .	ST BRIGIDS	132
HASLAM	1977, 85, 95.	KILTERNAN	112
HASTINGS	1974 .	ST BRIGIDS	145
HATCHELL	1905 .	KILTERNAN	54
HAWKES	1954, 79.	ST BRIGIDS	46
HAYDEN	1966, 91.	GLENCULLEN	87
HAYES	1921, 55, 56.	KILTERNAN	29
HEALY	1823 .	OLD CONNAUGHT	34
HEALY	1886 ?, 1914.	OLD CONNAUGHT	2
HEALY	1932 .	CONVENT	6
HELY	1939, 44.	KILTERNAN	167
HENDERSON	1983, 96.	ST BRIGIDS	167
HENDY	1921 .	KILTERNAN	58
HENNESSY	1895 .	CONVENT	25
HENRY	1877, 83.	BARRINGTONS	39
HENRY	1872, 76.	BARRINGTONS	38
HERRICK	1965, 66.	ST BRIGIDS	31
HICKEY	1926 .	RATHMICHAEL	74
HICKS	1903, 15, 16.	KILTERNAN	63
HIGGINS	1910, 20.	RATHMICHAEL	51
HIGGINS	1956, 58.	RATHMICHAEL	17
HIGHTON	1962, 79.	ST BRIGIDS	129

HILL	1846 .	ST BRIGIDS	178
HILL	1997 .	KILTERNAN	95
HILLAS	1870, 1923, 35, 55.	ST BRIGIDS	52
HILLIARD	1985 .	ST BRIGIDS	4
HILTON	1952, 56.	KILTERNAN	12
HOCARTY	1900, 27.	GLENCULLEN	74
HODDER	1933 .	KILTERNAN	34
HODGES	1950, 66, 80.	ST BRIGIDS	111
HOLDEN	? .	CONVENT	8
HOLLWEY	1988 .	ST BRIGIDS	235
HONE	1912 .	KILTERNAN	79
HOPKINS	1955, 65.	RATHMICHAEL	49
HORAN	1969 .	CONVENT	10
HORAN	1980, 87.	KILTERNAN	116
HOSGOOD	1988 .	ST BRIGIDS	234
HOURIGAN	1995 .	CONVENT	7
HOWARD	1976, 93.	KILTERNAN	130
HOWE	1976 .	ST BRIGIDS	13
HUDSON	1995 .	KILTERNAN	179
HUDSON	1988 .	KILTERNAN	97
HUDSON	1999 .	KILTERNAN	182
HUGHES	1799 .	OLD CONNAUGHT	10
HUGHES	1874, 75, 96.	ST BRIGIDS	204
HUGHES	1869, 71, 79, 1905.	GLENCULLEN	30
HUGHES	1994 .	ST BRIGIDS	73
HUGHES	1915 .	KILTERNAN	175
HUMPHREYS	1942, 49, 51.	ST BRIGIDS	261
HURLEY	1911, 15, 17, 31.	TULLY	17
HUTCHINSON	1954, 75, 76.	ST BRIGIDS	44
HUTCHINSON	1995 .	ST BRIGIDS	64
HUTCHINSON	1992 .	ST BRIGIDS	67
HUTCHISSON	1712 .	TULLY	10
IRVINE	1909 .	KILTERNAN	65
IRVINE	1895, 1913, 20.	KILTERNAN	73

JACKSON	1882, 1922.	GLENCULLEN	14
JACKSON	1936, 44.	ST BRIGIDS	99
JACKSON	1946.	RATHMICHAEL	53
JACKSON	1974.	ST BRIGIDS	100
JELLETT	1907, 25, 42, 74, 86.	KILTERNAN	173
JOHNSON	1990.	ST BRIGIDS	1
JOHNSON	1956, 65.	ST BRIGIDS	168
JOHNSTON	1870.	ST BRIGIDS	97
JOHNSTON	1956.	ST BRIGIDS	169
JOHNSTON	1998.	ST BRIGIDS	62
JOHNSTONE	1936.	ST BRIGIDS	241
JOLLEY	1990, 96.	KILTERNAN	102
JOLLEY	1919, 58, 69.	KILTERNAN	67
JOLLEY	1904.	KILTERNAN	99
JOLLY	1882, 94, 1915, 35, 53.	KILTERNAN	93
JOLLY	1860, 66, 1904, 05.	ST BRIGIDS	104
JOLLY	1872, 98.	ST BRIGIDS	225
JOLLY	1872, 78, 87, 90, 1912.	ST BRIGIDS	103
JONES	1845, 48, 56, 67, 79, 92.	ST BRIGIDS	102
JONES	1871, 72, 95.	ST BRIGIDS	75
JONES	1981.	ST BRIGIDS	6
JORDAN	1857, 60.	OLD CONNAUGHT	17
JORDAN	1808, 13.	OLD CONNAUGHT	18
JUDGE	1981, 95.	KILTERNAN	133
KAVANAGH	1949, 80.	RATHMICHAEL	10
KAVANAGH	1853.	CONVENT	17
KAVANAGH	1918.	OLD CONNAUGHT	9
KAVENAGH	1717.	ST BRIGIDS	57
KEARNEY	1854.	TULLY	35
KEARNS	1800.	ST BRIGIDS	61
KEATING	1815, 17.	OLD CONNAUGHT	29
KEEGAN	1894.	KILTERNAN	71
KEELEY	1903, 21, 29, 39, 75, 90, 95.	KILTERNAN	48
KEELEY	1878, 1906.	GLENCULLEN	7

KEELEY	1975 .	KILTERNAN	127
KEHOE	1900 .	CONVENT	16
KELLEHER	?,?,?.	RATHMICHAEL	3
KELLY	1924 .	KILTERNAN	68
KELLY	1899, 1950.	GLENCULLEN	125
KELLY	1856 .	CONVENT	15
KELLY	1821, 43.	RATHMICHAEL	19
KELLY	1814 .	OLD CONNAUGHT	19
KELLY	1808 .	RATHMICHAEL	50
KELLY	1886, 98.	TULLY	43
KELLY	1944, 48.	RATHMICHAEL	34
KELLY	1893 .	RATHMICHAEL	80
KELLY	1953 .	RATHMICHAEL	72
KELLY	1892, 1901.	RATHMICHAEL	71
KELLY	1835, 47, 48.	GLENCULLEN	136
KELLY	1827, 41, 49, 50, 1929, 37.	GLENCULLEN	15
KELLY	1847, 71, 79, 89.	GLENCULLEN	137
KENNEDY	?.	ST BRIGIDS	277
KENNEDY	1979, 89.	KILTERNAN	111
KENNEDY	1882 .	GLENCULLEN	19
KENNEDY	? .	OLD CONNAUGHT	26
KENNY	1809 ?, 17.	OLD CONNAUGHT	6
KENNY	1855, 75, 92, 95.	GLENCULLEN	50
KENNY	1928, 40, 46.	GLENCULLEN	83
KENNY	1889, 1905.	GLENCULLEN	49
KENNY	1916, 27.	GLENCULLEN	65
KENNY	1887, 1927.	GLENCULLEN	19
KENNY	1886, 99.	OLD CONNAUGHT	43
KERR	1928 ?, 31 ?.	GLENCULLEN	77
KEVANS	1871.	TULLY	40
KIDD	1960, 87.	ST BRIGIDS	133
KING	1861, 73.	OLD CONNAUGHT	10
KINSELLA	1944, 66.	GLENCULLEN	71
KINSELLA	1952, 58.	GLENCULLEN	64

KIRWAN	1831, 36, 43, 53, 59.	TULLY	32
KIRWAN	1870, 76, 78.	TULLY	32
KNOTT	1955 .	CONVENT	15
KNOWLES	1978, 81.	KILTERNAN	114
KNOWLES	1944, 59, 82, 92.	KILTERNAN	16
KNOX	1871, 86.	ST BRIGIDS	195
KUSS	1969, 96.	ST BRIGIDS	35
KYLE	1839, 53, 85.	ST BRIGIDS	193
LADLEY	1856, 66.	ST BRIGIDS	85
LAFFAN	1998 .	CONVENT	25
LAMBE	1850, 61, 68, 79.	RATHMICHAEL	7
LAMBERT	1895, 1911, 12, 52.	RATHMICHAEL	22
LAMBERT	1898.	TULLY	36
LARGE	1962, 82.	ST BRIGIDS	130
LARGE	1956, 85.	ST BRIGIDS	170
LARGE	1930, 41, 59, 89.	KILTERNAN	52
LARKIN	1998 .	KILTERNAN	135
LATTEN	1910 .	GLENCULLEN	126
LAVELLE	1924 .	KILTERNAN	61
LAW	1891, 1921.	GLENCULLEN	17
LAWLESS	? .	OLD CONNAUGHT	35
LAWLESS	1883, 84.	RATHMICHAEL	77
LEADBEATER	1843 .	BARRINGTONS	4
LEARY	1864 .	GLENCULLEN	5
LEE	1947, 53.	RATHMICHAEL	31
LEE	1902, 07, 18.	RATHMICHAEL	73
LEESON	1813 .	OLD CONNAUGHT	36
LEMAN	1880 .	BLACKROCK	1
LENEHAN	1894, 98, 1944, 94.	GLENCULLEN	41
LENEHAN	1862, 70, 1919, 44, 77.	GLENCULLEN	40
LEONARD	1925, 43, 78.	RATHMICHAEL	23
LEONARD	1992 .	ST BRIGIDS	249
LEONARD	1941, 46, 74.	RATHMICHAEL	55
LEOPOLD	1991 .	ST BRIGIDS	269

LESLIE	1817, 20, 32, 44, 47, 79, 81.	ST BRIGIDS	198
LESTRANGE	1976, 83.	ST BRIGIDS	161
LEVINGSTON	1870 .	ST BRIGIDS	97
LEYNE	? .	GLENCULLEN	8
LICKEN	1938, 53, 61, 88.	GLENCULLEN	54
LICKEN	1917, 38.	GLENCULLEN	53
LINDSAY	1971 .	ST BRIGIDS	21
LOFTUS	1913 .	KILTERNAN	74
LUGGAR	1974, 84.	ST BRIGIDS	144
LYNCH	1890, 92, 93.	RATHMICHAEL	80
LYNCH	? .	RATHMICHAEL	81
LYNCH	1939 .	CONVENT	5
LYNCH	1880, 86, 98, 1902, 19, 27.	OLD CONNAUGHT	39
LYONS	1846 .	ST BRIGIDS	278
LYONS	1821, 69, 88, 89.	ST BRIGIDS	280
MacGREGOR	1976 .	ST BRIGIDS	2
MACILWAINE	1863, 78, 84, 1907.	ST BRIGIDS	89
MACKAY	1927, 36.	KILTERNAN	31
MACKENZIE	1970, 95, 96.	KILTERNAN	140
MACKEY	1876 .	CONVENT	11
MACKIE	1919 .	OLD CONNAUGHT	39
MacLAGAN	1855 .	ST BRIGIDS	187
MACNAMARA	1967 .	ST BRIGIDS	34
MADDEN	1993 .	KILTERNAN	108
MAGAWLY	1751 .	ST BRIGIDS	88
MAGEE	1909 .	RATHMICHAEL	48
MAGEE	? .	RATHMICHAEL	63
MAGEE	1877, 84, 87, 1909.	OLD CONNAUGHT	11
MAGEE	1858, 61, 77, 1900.	OLD CONNAUGHT	12
MAGILL	1981 .	ST BRIGIDS	12
MAGUIRE	1895, 1900, 28.	GLENCULLEN	119
MAGUIRE	1926, 56, 58, 65.	GLENCULLEN	20
MAGUIRE	1918, 25.	RATHMICHAEL	76
MAHER	1908 .	CONVENT	22

MAHER	1875, 97, 1911.	GLENCULLEN	110
MALAM	1830 .	ST BRIGIDS	92
MALONE	1871, 76.	BARRINGTONS	29
MALONE	1910 .	BARRINGTONS	28
MALONE	1904 .	BARRINGTONS	27
MALONE	1916 .	BARRINGTONS	24
MALONE	1905 .	BARRINGTONS	30
MALONE	1907 .	BARRINGTONS	26
MALONE	1974 .	BARRINGTONS	31
MALONE	1947 .	BARRINGTONS	32
MANDERS	1928 .	BARRINGTONS	23
MANSERAGH	1932, 35, 45.	KILTERNAN	159
MARA	1757 .	ST BRIGIDS	229
MARRABLE	1946 .	KILTERNAN	18
MARRABLE	1918, 40, 44.	KILTERNAN	45
MARTIN	1899, 1906.	GLENCULLEN	111
MARTIN	1946 .	CONVENT	4
MARTIN	1902 .	CONVENT	14
MASON	1805 .	ST BRIGIDS	211
MASON	1860, 82.	ST BRIGIDS	212
MASON	1895, 1911.	RATHMICHAEL	22
MASSEY	1862, 67, 88.	ST BRIGIDS	112
MAUNSELL	1858, 67, 68, 75, 79, 86.	ST BRIGIDS	58
McANANY	1876, 78, 81.	GLENCULLEN	48
McAVOY	1983 .	ST BRIGIDS	166
McBRIEN	1936, 56.	RATHMICHAEL	65
McCABE	?.	GLENCULLEN	118
McCABE	1810, 28.	TULLY	48
McCABE	1904, 12, 38.	GLENCULLEN	115
McCAFFREY	1913 .	CONVENT	6
McCAHEY	1901.	TULLY	22
McCANN	1921 .	GLENCULLEN	82
McCANN	1900, 19, 41.	GLENCULLEN	100
McCARTHY	1973 .	ST BRIGIDS	160

94

McCARTHY	1979 .	ST BRIGIDS	163
McCLUSKEY	1915, 22, 40.	GLENCULLEN	108
McCONNELL	1936, 40, 90, 92.	KILTERNAN	82
McCORMACK	1888 .	CONVENT	6
McCORMACK	1753 .	RATHMICHAEL	13
McCORMACK	1916 .	CONVENT	4
McCREEDY	1974, 88.	ST BRIGIDS	162
McDONAGH	1914 .	GLENCULLEN	109
McDONALD	1921, 48.	RATHMICHAEL	78
McDOWELL	1981 .	ST BRIGIDS	127
McENENY	1838, 39, 55, 59.	GLENCULLEN	47
McGARRY	1944, 87.	RATHMICHAEL	26
McGINN	1936 .	GLENCULLEN	120
McGOWAN	1927, 53, 57, 63, 94.	RATHMICHAEL	47
McGRATH	1885, 94, 96.	TULLY	6
McGRATH	1967 .	RATHMICHAEL	42
McGUINESS	1806, 09.	ST BRIGIDS	90
McGUIRE	1878, 92, 96, 1921.	GLENCULLEN	22
McGUIRE	1836, 37, 39.	GLENCULLEN	21
McHENRY	1969 .	CONVENT	11
McHOUL	1982, 95.	ST BRIGIDS	113
McILROY	1931 .	KILTERNAN	42
McKEON	1876 .	GLENCULLEN	34
McKEOWN	1929 .	CONVENT	12
McKINSTRY	1996 .	KILTERNAN	122
McLUSKY	1971 .	ST BRIGIDS	29
McMAHON	1970 .	CONVENT	21
McMANUS	1921 .	GLENCULLEN	132
McMANUS	1888 .	RATHMICHAEL	60
McMANUS	1856, 63, 70, 75, 1918.	GLENCULLEN	6
McMANUS	1903 ?, 21.	GLENCULLEN	131
McNALLY	1758 .	RATHMICHAEL	25
McNAMARA	?.	RATHMICHAEL	5
McNAMEE	1917, 24.	RATHMICHAEL	82

McPARTLAND	1990 .	CONVENT	19
McQUESTON	1976 .	ST BRIGIDS	18
MEARES	1792 .	ST BRIGIDS	217
MEATES	1971 .	ST BRIGIDS	15
MEATES	1972, 75.	ST BRIGIDS	22
MEDCALF	1835, 69, 77, 80.	ST BRIGIDS	185
MEDCALF	1955, 65, 70, 73.	ST BRIGIDS	48
MEGAN	1883.	KILTERNAN	86
MELLON	1963 .	ST BRIGIDS	119
MELLON	1966, 73.	ST BRIGIDS	33
MERCER	1795.	TULLY	23
MERCIER	1990 .	KILTERNAN	8
MEREDITH	1989 .	ST BRIGIDS	72
MERRIGAN	1915, 31.	GLENCULLEN	56
METCALFE	1986 .	CONVENT	28
MEYER	1965, 70.	KILTERNAN	150
MEYER	1967 .	KILTERNAN	149
MILEY	1898 .	CONVENT	26
MILLAR	? .	ST BRIGIDS	273
MILLER	1995 .	ST BRIGIDS	74
MILLER	1763, 1809, 18, 53.	ST BRIGIDS	193
MILLNER	1943, 63.	KILTERNAN	38
MILLS	1859, 61, 67, 75, 80, 84.	ST BRIGIDS	143
MINCHIN	1843, 84.	ST BRIGIDS	227
MINNITT	1818, 30.	ST BRIGIDS	176
MITCHELL	1964 .	ST BRIGIDS	37
MITCHELL	1936 .	KILTERNAN	174
MOFFITT	1985 .	ST BRIGIDS	247
MOLONEY	1965 .	CONVENT	28
MOLONEY	1849 .	ST BRIGIDS	182
MOLONY	1929 .	KILTERNAN	169
MOLONY	1938, 72, 85.	KILTERNAN	168
MONAGHAN	1871 .	RATHMICHAEL	48
MOORE	1924, 52, 54.	GLENCULLEN	94

MOORE	1826 .	OLD CONNAUGHT	1
MOORE	1849.	TULLY	24
MORAHAN	1943 .	CONVENT	1
MORAN	1849 .	CONVENT	16
MORGAN	?.	TULLY	8
MORGAN	1998 .	ST BRIGIDS	154
MORGAN	1958, 96.	ST BRIGIDS	136
MORRIS	1933, 49, 57.	ST BRIGIDS	91
MORROW	1960, 79.	ST BRIGIDS	82
MULLEN	?.	RATHMICHAEL	34
MULLIGAN	1895, 1942.	GLENCULLEN	59
MULLIGAN	1915, 33, 65.	GLENCULLEN	58
MULLIGAN	1915, 46, 58, 75.	GLENCULLEN	114
MULVEY	1945 .	GLENCULLEN	91
MURPHY	1927 .	CONVENT	15
MURPHY	1906, 20, 22.	GLENCULLEN	99
MURPHY	1821, 26.	OLD CONNAUGHT	1
MURPHY	1925 .	CONVENT	16
MURPHY	1910 .	OLD CONNAUGHT	14
MURPHY	1988, 90.	ST BRIGIDS	1
MURPHY	1931 .	OLD CONNAUGHT	38
MURPHY	1871, 72.	OLD CONNAUGHT	37
MURPHY	1827, 34, 52.	GLENCULLEN	16
MURPHY	1933 .	KILTERNAN	41
MURPHY	?, 1898.	RATHMICHAEL	21
MURPHY	1918, 24.	KILTERNAN	78
MURRAY	1848 .	ST BRIGIDS	279
MURRAY	1929, 59.	RATHMICHAEL	61
MURRAY	1919, 36.	RATHMICHAEL	69
MYERSCOUGH	1985, 96.	KILTERNAN	110
MYERSCOUGH	1927, 54.	KILTERNAN	165
NAYLOR	1931 .	KILTERNAN	163
NEELY	1907 .	KILTERNAN	80
NEIL	1850, 52, 68.	RATHMICHAEL	32

NELSON	1961 .	KILTERNAN	39
NELSON	1916, 26, 31.	KILTERNAN	166
NEWMAN	1964, 78.	ST BRIGIDS	116
NEWMAN	1980 .	ST BRIGIDS	115
NIXON	1854, 95, 1900, 02, 10.	ST BRIGIDS	197
NOLAN	1896, 1905, 08, 10, 30, 73.	GLENCULLEN	105
NOLAN	1951, 85.	RATHMICHAEL	87
NOLAN	1902 .	GLENCULLEN	112
NORTH	1859 .	ST BRIGIDS	109
O'BRIEN	1918, 54.	RATHMICHAEL	64
O'BRIEN	1990 .	CONVENT	12
O'BRIEN	1911, 12.	GLENCULLEN	106
O'BRIEN	1885 .	CONVENT	21
O'CONNELL-FITZSIMON	1884, 94, 1910, 39, 48, 53.	GLENCULLEN	8
O'CONNELL-FITZSIMON	1971 .	KILTERNAN	143
O'CONNELL-FITZSIMON	1901, 02.	GLENCULLEN	10
O'DOHERTY	1995 .	ST BRIGIDS	183
O'DONNELL	1945 .	CONVENT	13
O'GRADY	1938, 41, 45.	RATHMICHAEL	58
O'HALLORAN	1947 .	RATHMICHAEL	9
O'KEEFFE	1877 .	BLACKROCK	3
O'KEEFFE	1946 .	CONVENT	25
O'KEEFFE	1912 .	CONVENT	25
O'KELLY	1870 .	OLD CONNAUGHT	21
O'KELLY	1870, 71.	OLD CONNAUGHT	20
O'LEARY	1926 .	CONVENT	14
O'LEARY	1838 .	GLENCULLEN	29
O'MORCHOE	1970, 87.	KILTERNAN	138
O'MORCHOE	1918, 21, 24, 58, 62	KILTERNAN	78
O'MORCHOE	1973, 89, 95.	KILTERNAN	78
O'NEAL	1812 ?.	OLD CONNAUGHT	15
O'NEALE	1719 .	OLD CONNAUGHT	5
O'NEILL	1876 .	GLENCULLEN	102
O'NEILL	1847, 64, 77, 80.	GLENCULLEN	113

O'NEILL	1842, 52, 87, 1902, 20.	GLENCULLEN	103
O'NEILL	1974 .	BARRINGTONS	31
O'NEILL	1925, 44.	GLENCULLEN	84
O'NEILL	1920 .	GLENCULLEN	85
O'NEILL	1922 .	GLENCULLEN	75
O'REILLY	1899 .	CONVENT	28
O'REILLY	1897, 1900.	RATHMICHAEL	38
O'REILLY	1970 .	GLENCULLEN	42
O'REILLY	1885, 1907.	OLD CONNAUGHT	22
O'RORKE	1860, 68.	GLENCULLEN	2
O'ROURKE	1924, 34.	RATHMICHAEL	74
O'SULLIVAN	1940 .	CONVENT	3
O'TOOLE	1872, 73, 80.	OLD CONNAUGHT	13
O'TOOLE	1933 .	CONVENT	18
OLIVER	1971 .	KILTERNAN	142
ORMROD	1973, 78.	ST BRIGIDS	16
ORPEN	1953 .	ST BRIGIDS	50
ORR	1835 .	ST BRIGIDS	285
ORR	? .	ST BRIGIDS	273
OVEREND	1969 .	KILTERNAN	151
PALMER	1965 .	ST BRIGIDS	38
PARKINSON	1971 .	ST BRIGIDS	42
PARNELL	1877 .	LOUGHLINSTOWN	5
PATEY	1919 .	KILTERNAN	176
PATTERSON	1996 .	ST BRIGIDS	141
PEACOCKE	1936, 50 ?.	ST BRIGIDS	270
PEACOCKE	1837, 44, 51 ?, 71, 73, 85.	ST BRIGIDS	198
PEACOCKE	1901, 11, 20, 29.	ST BRIGIDS	198
PEDLOW	1999 .	KILTERNAN	181
PETIT	1898 .	CONVENT	27
PEYTON	1892 .	CONVENT	24
PHEIFER	1992 .	KILTERNAN	106
PHELAN	1968 .	CONVENT	19
PHELAN	1923 .	CONVENT	3

PHELAN	1914 .	CONVENT	26
PHELAN	1929 .	CONVENT	10
PHILLIPS	1975 .	KILTERNAN	126
PHILLIPS	1848, 61, 1903, 36, 51, 69.	ST BRIGIDS	105
PHIPPS	1834 .	ST BRIGIDS	182
PIERCE	1916 .	GLENCULLEN	66
PIERCE	1978 .	KILTERNAN	113
PILKINGTON	1981 .	KILTERNAN	117
PILLOW	1988, 92.	KILTERNAN	105
PIM	1900 .	BARRINGTONS	5
POLAND	1868 .	ST BRIGIDS	219
PONTET	1834 .	ST BRIGIDS	181
POTTER	1969, 88.	ST BRIGIDS	159
POTTS	1998 .	ST BRIGIDS	71
POTTS	1731.	TULLY	44
POWER	1970 .	KILTERNAN	4
POWER	? .	GLENCULLEN	123
POWER	1938 .	CONVENT	11
POWER	1953 .	CONVENT	17
PRESTON	1975, 82.	ST BRIGIDS	17
PRINGLE	1998 .	KILTERNAN	148
PURCELL	1885 .	CONVENT	29
PURCELL	1901 .	CONVENT	17
PURNELL-EDWARDS	1956 .	ST BRIGIDS	157
RATH	1994 .	ST BRIGIDS	107
REID	1977 .	ST BRIGIDS	184
REID	1838, 58.	RATHMICHAEL	37
REILLY	1831, 54, 61.	GLENCULLEN	42
REILLY	1828.	TULLY	15
REYNOLDS	1843, 54, 1907.	TULLY	38
RICHARDS	1931, 38.	ST BRIGIDS	60
RICHARDSON	1992 .	KILTERNAN	106
RICHARDSON	1952 .	KILTERNAN	12
RICHARDSON	1933, 65, 66.	RATHMICHAEL	84

RICHMOND	1942 .	RATHMICHAEL	68
RICKETTS	? .	ST BRIGIDS	261
RIDGLEY	1786 .	ST BRIGIDS	57
RINKLE	1852, 78, 96.	GLENCULLEN	1
RIORDAN	1981 .	GLENCULLEN	32
RIVAZ	1952, 75.	ST BRIGIDS	43
ROBERTS	1933, 35.	KILTERNAN	34
ROBERTS	1938 .	KILTERNAN	35
ROBERTS	1901, 17, 30, 39.	KILTERNAN	69
ROBINSON	1760, 66.	TULLY	8
ROBINSON	1950, 57.	KILTERNAN	21
ROCHFORD	1901.	TULLY	22
ROE	1849 .	GLENCULLEN	33
ROE	1940, 82.	GLENCULLEN	68
ROE	1916, 18, 53, 75.	GLENCULLEN	69
ROE	1947, 77.	GLENCULLEN	62
ROE	1919, 26, 39, 51, 58 ?.	GLENCULLEN	135
ROE	1865, 67.	GLENCULLEN	4
ROE	1864, 90, 91.	GLENCULLEN	5
ROGERS	1931 .	KILTERNAN	36
ROOKE	1823, 66, 83, 86, ?.	ST BRIGIDS	264
RORKE	?,?.	TULLY	35
ROSS	1980, 94.	ST BRIGIDS	126
ROSS	1979, 89.	ST BRIGIDS	125
ROSS	1990 .	KILTERNAN	10
ROSS	1985, 96.	ST BRIGIDS	246
ROULSTON	1984 .	ST BRIGIDS	251
ROWLAND	1954, 57, 87.	ST BRIGIDS	45
RUNDELL	1857, 89, 92, 1909.	ST BRIGIDS	55
RUSSELL	1947, 55, 56.	KILTERNAN	5
RUTHERFOORD	1918 .	KILTERNAN	170
RUTHERFOORD	1918, 41, 88.	KILTERNAN	171
RUTHERFOORD	1916, 38, 73.	KILTERNAN	172
RUTTLEDGE	1976, 82.	KILTERNAN	129

101

RYAN	1949 .	CONVENT	8
RYAN	1874 .	BLACKROCK	2
RYAN	1926, 32, 51, 56.	GLENCULLEN	128
RYAN	1832, 49, 67, 85.	TULLY	34
RYAN	1941 .	CONVENT	7
RYAN	1965 .	ST BRIGIDS	39
RYLANDS	1959, 65.	RATHMICHAEL	33
RYLANDS	1982 .	RATHMICHAEL	2
SALLEY	1923, 24, 30.	GLENCULLEN	31
SALLEY	1917, 19, 22.	GLENCULLEN	75
SARRATT	1982, 85.	ST BRIGIDS	14
SAVAGE	1907, 22.	RATHMICHAEL	83
SAVAGE	1951, 88.	GLENCULLEN	128
SAVAGE	1989, 94.	KILTERNAN	103
SCALES	1995 .	ST BRIGIDS	70
SCANLON	1978 .	KILTERNAN	157
SCANLON	1967, 89.	KILTERNAN	152
SCOTT	1892, 97, 1927, 52, 62, 74.	ST BRIGIDS	280
SCOVELL	1851, 53, 61, 75.	ST BRIGIDS	177
SEGRAVE	1858 .	CONVENT	19
SHARP	1856 .	ST BRIGIDS	192
SHARPE	1899 .	LOUGHLINSTOWN	3
SHARPE	1986 .	ST BRIGIDS	8
SHAW	1969 .	ST BRIGIDS	28
SHEA	1879.	TULLY	29
SHEA	1762 .	ST BRIGIDS	95
SHEILL	1952 .	KILTERNAN	40
SHERMAN	?,?,?.	TULLY	3
SHERRY	1794, 1829.	TULLY	11
SHERWOOD	1886 .	KILTERNAN	84
SHIELL	1986, 89.	ST BRIGIDS	245
SHOLEDICE	1991 .	KILTERNAN	104
SHORTT	1885, 1901, 12.	OLD CONNAUGHT	23
SIEVEWRIGHT	1993 .	KILTERNAN	107

SIMMONS	1971, 83.	ST BRIGIDS	30
SITMELL	1866.	KILTERNAN	75
SKELTON	1913, 19, 21.	OLD CONNAUGHT	3
SKELTON	1919.	OLD CONNAUGHT	4
SKERRITT	1987, 95.	ST BRIGIDS	233
SKINNER	1957.	ST BRIGIDS	155
SLACKE ?	1895.	RATHMICHAEL	67
SMEATON-COUSE	1990.	ST BRIGIDS	237
SMITH	1925.	KILTERNAN	31
SMITH	1986	ST BRIGIDS	243
SMITH	1909.	KILTERNAN	55
SMITH	1994.	RATHMICHAEL	52
SMITH	1984 ?.	ST BRIGIDS	252
SMYTH	1845, 50, 73.	ST BRIGIDS	263
SMYTH	1831.	ST BRIGIDS	202
SMYTH	1860.	GLENCULLEN	96
SMYTH	1809, 31, 41, 51, 89.	ST BRIGIDS	101
SMYTH	1795, 1802, 06.	ST BRIGIDS	205
SMYTH	1814, 15, 88.	ST BRIGIDS	205
SOMERS	1942.	KILTERNAN	30
SPENCER	1955, 63, 75.	ST BRIGIDS	173
SPENCER	1977, 79, 97.	ST BRIGIDS	148
SPOLENS	1904.	CONVENT	12
SPOOR	1996.	ST BRIGIDS	63
SPRENGEL	1958, 69.	ST BRIGIDS	152
St. LAWRENCE	1859.	ST BRIGIDS	207
STANFORD	1868, 69.	ST BRIGIDS	83
STAPLETON	1799, 1806 ?, 08.	ST BRIGIDS	216
STAUNTON	1895, 96.	TULLY	9
STAUNTON	1835, 68, 69, 72, 73, 84.	TULLY	42
STEVENS	1945.	KILTERNAN	27
STEVENSON	1902, 12, 18, 41, 45.	KILTERNAN	89
STEVENSON	1968, 93.	KILTERNAN	155
STEVENSON	1884.	KILTERNAN	88

STEVENSON	1928, 59.	KILTERNAN	83
STEWART	1950, 65, 69.	KILTERNAN	11
STOKES	1876 .	GLENCULLEN	88
STOREY	1952, 61.	KILTERNAN	2
STOREY	1969, 70.	KILTERNAN	67
STRANGMAN	1895 .	BARRINGTONS	3
STREAN	1834, 35, 53, 61, 62, 66.	ST BRIGIDS	201
STREET	1956, 69.	ST BRIGIDS	171
STRINGER	1977, 83.	ST BRIGIDS	124
STRONG	1886.	KILTERNAN	75
STUART	1846 .	ST BRIGIDS	56
SUTTON	1906, 18, 25, 36.	KILTERNAN	72
SUTTON	1946, 49, 52.	KILTERNAN	17
SUTTON	1918, 22.	KILTERNAN	59
SUTTON	1903, 37.	KILTERNAN	70
SUTTON	1884, 90.	KILTERNAN	87
SUTTON	1971, 96.	KILTERNAN	141
SUTTON	1956 .	KILTERNAN	77
SUTTON	1910 .	OLD CONNAUGHT	14
SYMINGTON	1975 .	ST BRIGIDS	146
TALBOT	1958 .	CONVENT	2
TALBOT	1995 .	KILTERNAN	96
TALBOT	1972, 81.	KILTERNAN	146
TANNANY ?	1756 ?.	TULLY	25
TARBET	1821, 34, 36.	ST BRIGIDS	280
TATE	1985, 97.	KILTERNAN	132
TAYLOR	1885, 94, 1912, 13, 21, 58.	KILTERNAN	74
THOMAS	1980 .	RATHMICHAEL	10
THOMAS	1955, 78.	ST BRIGIDS	172
THOMAS	1922, 59.	GLENCULLEN	81
THOMPSON	1951, 63, 90.	KILTERNAN	8
THOMPSON	1875, 81.	RATHMICHAEL	85
THOMSON	1974 .	KILTERNAN	147
THORP	1964 .	ST BRIGIDS	118

THWAITES	1834 ?, 75 ?, 7?, 83.	ST BRIGIDS	286
THWAITES	1836, 82, 89 ?.	ST BRIGIDS	284
TIGHE	1885 .	CONVENT	22
TOMLINSON	1951 .	KILTERNAN	49
TOOKEY	1814 ?.	ST BRIGIDS	262
TOOLE	? .	OLD CONNAUGHT	3
TOOLE	1857 .	GLENCULLEN	98
TOPPING	1989 .	KILTERNAN	25
TOWNSEND	1974 .	KILTERNAN	124
TRACEY	1974, 78, 80.	KILTERNAN	125
TRACEY	1932, 77.	KILTERNAN	32
TRACEY	1971, 73.	KILTERNAN	144
TRACEY	1976, 83.	KILTERNAN	128
TRACEY	1904, 09, 11, 19, 42.	KILTERNAN	100
TRACEY	1967, 71, 96.	KILTERNAN	154
TRACEY	1996 .	KILTERNAN	122
TRACEY	1889, 91, 93, 1910, 24, 47.	KILTERNAN	94
TRACEY	1934, 72, 99.	KILTERNAN	33
TRAINOR	1899, 1901, 02, 03.	RATHMICHAEL	1
TRAVERS	1897, 1914, 19, 23, 29, 31..	GLENCULLEN	70
TRAVERS	1942, 45 51.	GLENCULLEN	70
TRINDER	1973 .	ST BRIGIDS	41
TROUGHTON-SMITH	1986 .	ST BRIGIDS	243
TUBBS	1804 .	ST BRIGIDS	208
TUFNELL	1901 .	ST BRIGIDS	198
TURPIN	1983 .	ST BRIGIDS	137
TUTTY	1996 .	KILTERNAN	141
UARDON	? .	ST BRIGIDS	199
VANCE	1810 .	ST BRIGIDS	189
VANDERKISTE	1995 .	KILTERNAN	112
VAUX	1996 .	ST BRIGIDS	243
VERSCHOYLE	1810 .	ST BRIGIDS	56
VINCENT	1994 .	ST BRIGIDS	65
WAKEFIELD	1902 .	BARRINGTONS	9

WALDRON	1869, 71.	ST BRIGIDS	214
WALE	1859, 60.	ST BRIGIDS	86
WALKER	1934.	KILTERNAN	90
WALKER	1863, 54, 58.	RATHMICHAEL	46
WALKER	1952, 53, 59, 82.	KILTERNAN	22
WALKER	1955, 80,.	KILTERNAN	23
WALKER	1959.	ST BRIGIDS	140
WALLIS	1936.	KILTERNAN	36
WALSH	1966.	CONVENT	16
WALSH	1866, 75, 1900, 24.	GLENCULLEN	46
WALSH	?.	GLENCULLEN	117
WALSH	1939, 50, 95.	GLENCULLEN	122
WALSH	1940, 47.	GLENCULLEN	138
WALSH	1879.	GLENCULLEN	45
WALSH	1971.	CONVENT	3
WALSH	1914.	RATHMICHAEL	57
WALSH	1912.	OLD CONNAUGHT	23
WALSH	1980.	ST BRIGIDS	27
WALSH	1755.	TULLY	50
WALSH	1917.	GLENCULLEN	73
WALSH	1933, 51.	GLENCULLEN	76
WALSH	1756.	OLD CONNAUGHT	8
WARBURTON	1828, 60, 73, 1910.	ST BRIGIDS	265
WARD	1917, 21.	GLENCULLEN	80
WARDLAW	1974, 76, 84.	ST BRIGIDS	23
WARNER	1830.	ST BRIGIDS	92
WATERS	1933, 58.	RATHMICHAEL	43
WATERS	1929, 32, 34, 46.	RATHMICHAEL	53
WATERS	1900.	CONVENT	2
WATSON	1866.	ST BRIGIDS	259
WATSON	1980.	KILTERNAN	115
WATTS	1871, 89.	ST BRIGIDS	106
WEBLEY	1867.	ST BRIGIDS	257
WESTON	1768.	ST BRIGIDS	228

WHATELY	1860 .	ST BRIGIDS	86
WHEELER	1984, 93.	ST BRIGIDS	66
WHELAN	1820, 27.	TULLY	15
WHELAN	1877 .	CONVENT	10
WHELAN	1979 .	CONVENT	23
WHELAN	1947 .	CONVENT	22
WHELAN	1944, 57, 81.	RATHMICHAEL	35
WHITE	1876 .	ST BRIGIDS	196
WILLIAMSON	1990 .	ST BRIGIDS	236
WILLIS	1919, 39, 75.	KILTERNAN	46
WILLIS	1968, 87.	KILTERNAN	51
WILLIS	1955 ?, 81 ?.	KILTERNAN	47
WILLIS	1968, 93.	KILTERNAN	20
WILLIS	1954, 58, 71, 74.	KILTERNAN	19
WILLIS	1927, 54 .	KILTERNAN	49
WILSON	1914, 31, 36.	KILTERNAN	174
WILSON	1926 .	KILTERNAN	44
WILSON	1928 ?, 55 ?, 66.	KILTERNAN	13
WINDER	1873, 75, 1912, 39.	ST BRIGIDS	210
WINDER	1880, 94.	ST BRIGIDS	211
WOODMAN	1973, 85.	ST BRIGIDS	250

OTHER PUBLISHED MEMORIAL INSCRIPTIONS
OF
DUN LAOGHAIRE RATHDOWN COUNTY.

CARRICKBRENNAN, Monkstown:
Irish Genealogist Vol.4, No.3, 1970 and Vol.4 No.4, 1971.

St BEGNET'S, Dalkey:
Irish Genealogist Vol.5 No.2, 1995.

DEANS GRANGE, Co. Dublin
Dun Laoghaire Genealogical Society:
Vol.1. South West Section, 1994.
Vol.2. Lower North Section ,1997.
Vol.3. Upper North Section, 1998.
Vol.4. South Section, 2000.

KILGOBBIN (Old):
Memorials of the Dead; Dublin City & County, No.2.

KILGOBBIN (New):
Memorials of the Dead; Dublin City & County No.3.

KILL O' THE GRANGE, St Fintan's:
Irish Genealogist Vol.4 No.5, 1972.

KILLINEY (Old):
Irish Genealogist Vol.4 No.6, 1973.

KILTERNAN (Old): Bishop's Lane:
Memorials of the Dead; Dublin City & County, No.2.

TANEY, St Nathi's, Dundrum:
The Parish of Taney: a history of Dundrum,
by F.E. Ball & E. Hamilton, 1895.

Society Publications

website ordering on *http://welcome.to/GenealogyIreland*

QUARTERLY JOURNAL of the GENEALOGICAL SOCIETY of IRELAND
The Journal (ISSN - pending) price IR£3.50 - members IR£3.00 (postage IR£1.00 Ireland & UK - elsewhere IR£2.00) Editor: **Liam Mac Alasdair** - E-mail: Lmac@dna.ie **(IR£16.00 - four issues by mail to Ireland & UK: IR£20.00 elsewhere)**

The Genie Gazette
This is the Society's monthly newsletter (ISSN 1393-3183). It is available free of charge. E-mail: **GenSocIreland@iol.ie**

DEANSGRANGE MEMORIAL INSCRIPTIONS
"Memorial Inscriptions of Deansgrange Cemetery, Blackrock, Co. Dublin, Ireland Vol 1 - South West Section" (ISBN 1 898471 20 07) price IR£6.00 (postage IR£1.00 Ireland & IR£2.00 overseas).. Co-ordinator: *Barry O'Connor*

"Memorial Inscriptions of Deansgrange Cemetery, Blackrock, Co. Dublin, Ireland Vol. 2 Lower North Section" (ISBN 1 898471 30 4) price IR£7.00 (postage IR£1.00 Ireland & IR£2.00 overseas). Co-ordinator: *Barry O'Connor.*

"Memorial Inscriptions of Deansgrange Cemetery, Blackrock, Co. Dublin, Ireland Vol. 3 Upper North Section" (ISBN 1 898471 55 X) price IR£7.00 (postage IR£1.00 Ireland and IR£2.00 overseas).. Co-ordinator: *Barry O'Connor.*

"Memorial Inscriptions of Deansgrange Cemetery, Blackrock, Co. Dublin, Ireland Vol. 4 South Section" (ISBN 1 898471 51 7) price IR£9.00 (postage IR£1.00 Ireland and IR£3.00 overseas). Co-ordinator: *Barry O'Connor.*

IRISH GENEALOGICAL SOURCES SERIES
Irish Genealogical Sources No. 1 "Shillelagh & Ballinacor South, Co. Wicklow 1837 - A Memorial" (ISBN 1 898471 40 1) price IR£5.00 (postage IR£1.00 - Ireland & IR£2.00 overseas).. Compiled & Edited by *Seán Magee.*

Irish Genealogical Sources No. 2 "Corn Growers, Carriers & Traders, County Wicklow 1788, 1789 & 1790" (ISBN 1 898471 50 9). price IR£3.00 (postage IR£1.00 - Ireland & IR£2.00 overseas).. Compiled by *George H. O'Reilly & James O. Coyle.*

Irish Genealogical Sources No. 3 "Newcastle, County Wicklow - School Register 1864-1947" (ISBN 1 898471 70 3) price IR£7.00 (postage IR£1.00 - Ireland & IR£2.00 overseas). *George H. O'Reilly*

Irish Genealogical Sources No. 4 "Croasdaile's History of Rosenallis, Co. Laois, Ireland" (ISBN 1 898471 10 X) price IR£5.00 (postage IR£1.00 - Ireland & IR£2.00 overseas) Edited by *Michael Merrigan*.

Irish Genealogical Sources No. 5 "Dublin City 1901 - Census Index to the North Strand, Clonliffe Road & Summerhill District" (ISBN 1 898471 75 4) price IR£5.00 (postage IR£1.00 - Ireland & IR£2.00 overseas). Extracted and indexed by *Marie Keogh*.

Irish Genealogical Sources No. 6 "Booterstown, Co. Dublin, Ireland - School Registers 1861-1872 & 1891-1939" (ISBN 1 898471 80 0) price IR£7.00 (postage IR£1.00 Ireland & IR£2.50 overseas) Compiled by *Frieda Carroll*.

Irish Genealogical Sources No. 7 "Dublin Street Index 1798 *extracted from* Whitelaw's Census" (ISBN 1 898471 85 1) by **Seán Magee** (Price: IR£3.00 - p+p IR£1.00 Ireland & UK : IR£2.00 others) *Seán Magee*.

Irish Genealogical Sources No. 8 "Weavers of Prosporous, County Kildare, Balbriggan, County Dublin and Tullamore, County Offaly in Memorials of 1826" (ISBN 1 898471 90 8) by **Seán Magee** (Price IR£3.00 p+p IR£1.00 Ireland & UK. IR£2.00 others)

Irish Genealogical Sources No. 9 "Petitioners Against Closure of Kill O' The Grange Cemetery, Co. Dublin, 1864" (ISBN 1 898471 95 9) by **Annette McDonnell** (Price IR£7.00 p+p IR£1.00 Ireland & UK. IR£2.00 others)

Irish Genealogical Sources No. 10 "Baldoyle, County Dublin 1901 Census Extracts" by *Marie Keogh*. Price IR£2.00 plus .50p p+p Ireland & UK and IR£1.00 elsewhere. (ISBN 1 898471 01 0)

Irish Genealogical Sources No. 11 "Harold (Boys) School, Glasthule, County Dublin - Registers 1904 - 1948" compiled by *Dr. Eithne Guilfoyle*. Price IR£9.00 plus IR£1.00 p+p Ireland & UK : IR£2.00 elsewhere. (ISBN 1 898471 06 1).

Irish Genealogical Sources No. 12 "The Irish Independence Movement on Tyneside 1919-1921" (ISBN 1 898471 11 8) price *Euro*4.00 (IR£3.15) (postage Ireland & UK *Euro*1.27 (IR£1.00) others *Euro*2.54 (IR£2.00) compiled by *Mary A. Barrington*. The Society published this volume to commemorate the 80th anniversary of the First Dáil (Irish Parliament) and the Declaration of Irish Independence on the 21st January 1919.

Irish Genealogical Sources No. 13 "St. Patrick's School, Dalkey, County Dublin - School Registers 1894-1970" (ISBN 1 898471 16 9) price *Euro*7.00 (IR£5.50) (postage Ireland & UK *Euro*1.27 (IR£1.00) others *Euro*2.54 (IR£2.00) compiled by *Annette McDonnell*.

Irish Genealogical Sources No. 14 "The People of the Rebellion - Wicklow 1798" (ISBN 1 898471 26 6) Price Ir£8.00 (p+p Ireland Ir£1.00 and others surface mail Ir£2.00 - airmail Ir£4.00) compiled by *Pat Power.*

Irish Genealogical Sources No. 15 "Officers & Recruits of the Louth Rifles 1854-1876" (ISBN 1 898471 31 2) Price Ir£8.00 (p+p Ireland Ir£1.00 and others surface mail Ir£2.00 - airmail Ir£4.00) compiled by *Brendan Hall.*

Irish Genealogical Sources No. 16 "Kilcoole County Wicklow, School Registers from 1861" (ISBN 1 898471 36 3) Price Ir£5.00 (p+p Ireland Ir£1.00 and others surface mail Ir£2.00 - airmail Ir£4.00) compiled by *George H. O'Reilly.*

Irish Genealogical Sources No.17 "Index to the 1821 Census of Crosserlough, Co. Cavan" (ISBN 1 898471 41 X) Price Ir£9.00 (p+p Ireland Ir£1.00 and others surface mail Ir£2.00 - airmail Ir£4.00) compiled by *Marie Keogh.*

Irish Genealogical Sources No. 18 "Dublin's Riviera in the Mid 19th. Century" ISBN 1 898471 46 0 Price IR£5.00 (p+p Ireland Ir£1.00 and others surface mail Ir£2.00 - airmail Ir£4.00) . Compiled by *Brendan Hall & George H. O'Reilly*

Other Publications

"Weavers & Related Trades, Dublin 1826 - A Genealogical Source" (ISBN 1 898471 15 0) price IR£5.00 (postage IR£1.00 Ireland & IR£2.00 overseas). *Seán Magee*

"A Guide to the Articles and Sources Published by the Dun Laoghaire Genealogical Society 1992 - 1996" (ISBN 1 898471 45 2) price IR£2.00 (postage IR£1.00). Compiled & Edited by *Brian Smith.* (out of print)

Genealogical Society of Ireland

(formerly Dun Laoghaire Genealogical Society)

The Genealogical Society of Ireland is a voluntary organisation with state registered charity status and is not a commercial research agency.

The Society is devoted to the promotion of genealogy and local history as an open access educational/leisure activity available to all. It publishes a monthly broadsheet, quarterly Journal, the Irish Genealogical Sources series and Cemetery memorial inscriptions.

Membership and further information on publications can be obtained from the Honorary Secretary at -

Genealogical Society of Ireland
11 Desmond Avenue
Dun Laoghaire
Co. Dublin
Ireland

Email address: GenSocIreland@iol.ie.
Website : http://welcome.to/GenealogyIreland